# A NEW ZEALAND CYCLE TOURING GUIDE

# PEDAL'
# PARA1

## NORTH ISLAND

### NIGEL RUSHTON

© 1996-2005
Dab Hand Publishing
Christchurch
New Zealand

First published: March 1996
Second edition: September 2001
1st reprint (including updates): August 2002
2nd reprint (including updates): September 2003
3rd reprint (including updates): August 2004
4th reprint (including updates): August 2005
5th reprint (including updates): August 2006

ISBN  0 - 473 - 07952 - 6

MAPS COURTESY of LAND INFORMATION NEW ZEALAND
CROWN COPYRIGHT RESERVED.

I would like to say a special thank you to all the people who have helped
in one way or another, voluntary and involuntarily!
Especially Bob & Raylee Price, Katrina Hope, Yumi Sako,
Mark and Sue Dumble, Bruce and Margaret O'Haloran,
Wouter Wagemakers and Annie Tiekstra,
Tired Old Tyke! (alias Victor Harry Greatorex)
Bob Regnault and Bob Adair.

Also a thank you to:
NIWA for wind characteristics
Michelle Edge of ARC and
all the staff at visitor information centres.

# CONTENTS: NORTH ISLAND

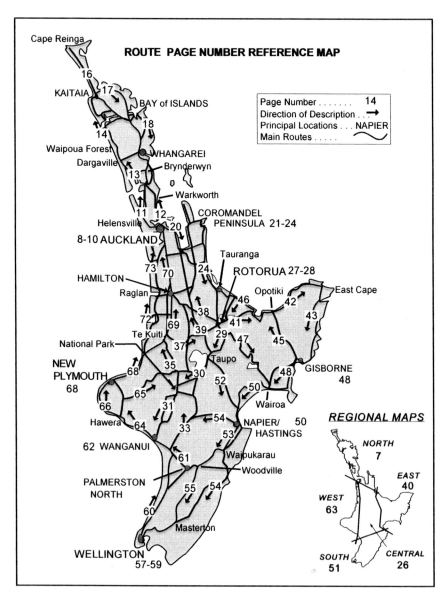

ROUTE PAGE NUMBER REFERENCE MAP

Cape Reinga

16

KAITAIA 17

BAY of ISLANDS

18

14

Waipoua Forest
Dargaville

WHANGAREI

Brynderwyn

13

Warkworth

11 12

Helensville 20

COROMANDEL
PENINSULA 21-24

8-10 AUCKLAND

Tauranga

73 70 24

ROTORURA 27-28

HAMILTON

Raglan

Opotiki

East Cape

46

42

72

38

69

41

43

Te Kuiti

39 29

45

National Park

37 47

NEW
PLYMOUTH
68

68

35

Taupo

30

52

48

GISBORNE
48

65

31

50

66

Wairoa

Hawera 64

33

54

NAPIER/ 50
HASTINGS

53

62 WANGANUI

61

Waipukarau

Woodville

PALMERSTON
NORTH

55 54

60

Masterton

WELLINGTON
57-59

**Page Number** . . . . . . 14
**Direction of Description** . . →
**Principal Locations** . . . NAPIER
**Main Routes** . . . . .

*REGIONAL MAPS*

*NORTH*
7

*EAST*
40

*WEST*
63

*SOUTH*
51

*CENTRAL*
26

# INTRODUCTION

**ABOUT THIS GUIDE** The purpose of this book is to provide a concise, practical and (hopefully) easy to follow guide for cycle tourers of New Zealand's North Island. The intention is to inform the users while still leaving something for them to discover.

**NEW:** Probably the most radical change to this edition is a quick reference map that has replaced the Table of Contents, mainly because it is much easier to locate the required page.

Other changes is an improvement to the maps, general text editing and moving some routes to new locations or redirecting them. Also this introduction is in two columns instead of one.

**REGIONS:** There are five regions as follows:
**NORTH** of the island including Auckland City, Northland and Coromandel circuits.
**CENTRAL** includes Rotorua to Wanganui, Bulls and back up to Auckland.
**WEST** between Auckland and Wanganui via Hamilton and New Plymouth.
**SOUTH** of a line between Napier and Wanganui including Wellington, plus Napier to Taupo.
**EAST** of a line from Napier to Rotorua.

**MAPS:** Of the area covered are on the first page of each region. It includes routes, highways and some localities. Coastlines have been included this time as the author's computing ability is improving.... and I'm getting better!!

**SECTIONS:** Each region is divided into sections and contain the following:

**ROUTE:** The routes described are usually main highways, presumes them to be sealed and says so if they're not. When an ALTERNATIVE, SIDE TRIP or LINK ROAD to/from the main route is available, there is a brief mention here with a more detailed account later. Major OPTIONS have their own sub-section. Influencing where a reader stops for the night is not intended.

In most cases routes are in their logical regions, hopefully! The obvious exceptions is Taupo to Napier in South. This is to help the "flow" from one area of interest to another.

**PROFILE:** This is the side view of the route and is intended as a <u>rough guide</u> to the terrain. Distances in kilometres, elevation in metres. The steepness is exaggerated due to the distances covered, don't be put off! Only a selection of localities are shown, with a few places in between being indicated by a letter, which corresponds with one in Services.

**SERVICES:** Indicate what to expect in a location in terms of information, food, accommodation, cycle shop and sometimes transport. Most providers are open 7 days. The following brief definitions are for those new to NZ.

**FOOD: 1. DAIRY:** Is the smallest of food outlets. Usually found in suburbs or small locations. These outlets are similar to a corner shop or delicatessen. Sometimes they sell takeaways or other cooked food. This is the place to try the famous New Zealand ice cream. Yum!
**2. STORE:** Comes between a dairy and a supermarket. Often linked to a grocery discount chain like Four Square or Pricecutter. Sometimes closed Saturday afternoon and/or Sunday.
**3. SUPERMARKETS:** Like others worldwide, even their names may be the same. Usually the cheapest place to buy food, but only found in larger population centres.
**4. TAKEAWAYS:** Sell food to be taken away such as those great cycling comestibles; fish and chips. It is not recommended to sit inside and eat without permission!
**5. TEAROOMS:** or coffee shops/cafés. An inexpensive place to sit for lunch. Pots of tea are often good value. Ice cream and takeaways are usually available. Small rural ones may close on Monday or Tuesday.
**6. RESTAURANT:** Same as anywhere in the world, the most expensive of all food outlets.

**7. PUB:** Public house or tavern; licensed premises where alcoholic beverages are sold. These are sometimes combined with a restaurant and/or accommodation.

**ACCOMMODATION: 1. CAMPING:** there are three categories as follows:

**1a. DoC CAMPING:** Run by Department of Conservation. Often located in scenic reserves or national parks. Those adjacent to highways also make good rest stops. Basic facilities usually prevail such as long drop toilets, picnic tables and water. Most are "self registration" where users deposit fees in an honesty box.

**1b. DOMAIN CAMPING:** Local council operated and located on public land (Domain). Those with basic facilities have a small charge or donation. Some are not advertised and only found by asking locals. Those similar to regular motor camps are listed as such.

**1c. MOTOR CAMPS:** These are usually the most expensive camping. Facilities vary but communal kitchens and bathrooms are standard. Guests use their own bedding and cooking utensils but sometimes these can be hired. Many have cabins; small simple huts containing beds. Said to be the  best places to meet Kiwis. Sometimes a minimum two person charge applies, even for solo cyclists. Obviously such situations should to be questioned.

**2. HOSTELS:** Provide inexpensive communal accommodation. Dormitories, common-rooms, bathrooms and equipped kitchens are standard. Guests bring their own sleeping bag but often linen can be hired. They're useful for up-to-date information. Some hostels allow camping. Some small hostels close in the off-season. There are two basic types of hostel:

**2a. BACKPACKER** (or bkpr). Standards vary but BBH hostels are normally better than VIP. BBH has the BPP%, the results of their annual customer satisfaction survey.

**2b. YHA** run by Youth Hostels Association, membership card required. Standards fairly uniform but usually more expensive than backpacker hostels. Note: All known camping grounds & hostels are listed.

**3. MOTEL:** Are self contained units and often includes a equipped kitchen.

**4. HOTEL:** Is often a pub with accommodation attached, sometimes a modern motor lodge. Note: Some owner operated hotels, particularly in country areas, may close on Sunday.

**5. B & B:** A guest house, farmstay or homestay. Usually small intimate places providing bed & breakfast, sometimes with 5 beds or less. These are not normally listed in this guide. Local lists are available at visitor information centres.

**6. LODGE:** This is a difficult one. This term is used by every level of accommodation. Often a wide selection is available in the same complex.

**7. WWOOF:** Willing Workers On Organic Farms. A work exchange scheme usually more suited to cyclists on extended tours and those interested in growing food the healthy way. Not listed here.

**BICYCLE SHOP:** The name and address of all known shops are listed in the main text, except in the big cities, where a selection is made. There isn't room to list all shops at the back as in the South Island. If possible check addresses for current listings before making contact, some may have changed. In places with no bicycle shops the mechanic at the local auto repair centre (garage) may be able to help.

**TRANSPORT:** Information on this is limited. "Bus" refers to the large 40 seater type, these are generally more reliable, comfortable and expensive than shuttles. Also "Shuttles" are often faster and more frequent than the larger buses.

Most buses and shutttles will take bikes, usually for a fixed fee regardless of distance travelled, but subject to available space. Bikes sometimes go separately from their owners. Some buses may also charge to take bike trailers.

**GRADIENTS:** This attempts to describe what sort of terrain to expect. Flat, undulating, rolling and steep are the basic variants. "Quite" or "fairly steep" is less steep than "steep" and "very steep". "Mostly flat" means at most a few minor rises and falls. "Undulates or rolls uphill" means the climb can vary with some short descents.

Variable steep" means expect the gradient to vary and I have no idea what "gradual up or down" means! Confused? So am I, it must be time for a cup of tea.

Gradients are probably the hardest part of the guide to get right. Wind, personal fitness and the bike's load are important factors when assessing the degree of difficulty. I have presumed the reader is reasonably fit. When battling a headwind it is common to think you're going uphill only to find it's an optical and cyclogical delusion! Not all hills are listed, sorry.

**ATTRACTIONS:** Include popular or unusual sights or activities an area has to offer, like swim with dolphins, tramping, sea kayaking and sheep-spotting. Boring activities such as golf, tennis etc are usually omitted. Fishing is possible almost anywhere there is water although it is not always mentioned. A valid licence is required.

**OPTIONS:** Are an **ALTERNATIVE** route, **SIDE TRIP** up a no exit or **LINK ROAD** to another major highway that may be worth considering, subject to the reader's preference and available time. Major options have there own sub-section, minor ones are listed under Options.

**STREET MAPS & DIRECTIONS:** and arterial route maps are only in Auckland, Rotorua & Wellington sections. They provide information for getting into and out of the cities and replace Route. The easiest routes are described and take to account of how busy they are. Cycling on motorways is prohibited on most but not all North Island motorways.

**MISCELLANEOUS: WEATHER:** This is the third most important thing in the entire Universe, after Pedallers' Paradise and a bike. NZ has a predominantly maritime climate and obviously it can only be described in general terms. Like weather everywhere it is largely unpredictable, which renders the next paragraph a waste of time.

Anyway, temperate climate predominates. The west has the most rainfall, Mt Egmont has recorded up to 11 metres! The Central high country tends to be the driest but is sometimes plagued by strong westerly winds that can blow intermittently for weeks. The East Coast has the most sunshine and doesn't usually suffer the

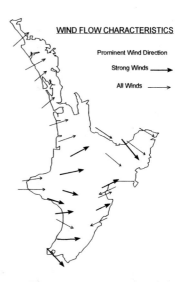

WIND FLOW CHARACTERISTICS

Prominent Wind Direction

Strong Winds ⟶

All Winds ⟶

extremes of other areas, but can be hit by the odd tropical storm or cyclone.

Spring and autumn are generally said to be the best times to tour in terms of lower temperatures, smaller crowds and variety of hues. Unfortunately these seasons are susceptible to long periods of unsettled and windy weather, especially after the equinox. Mid summer can be very hot and humid. February and March are reputedly the best months for long settled spells. In other words "good luck"!

Winter cycle touring is possible for the well equipped but remember, wet gear takes longer to dry. Apart from Desert Road, it is rare even for alpine pass highways to close for more than a couple of days due to snow.

Weather forecasts are usually quite accurate but often get the days wrong! Those who carry a radio can hear a 5 day long-range forecast at 12:30pm everyday on National Radio. This advert free station is accessible from most of NZ but reception in some remote areas is poor. As a bonus it also provides the best national and international news coverage!!

**MAPS:** This guide can be used independently but an additional map is recommended. NZ Tourism produce a general give-away map of New Zealand with some useful addresses. The Automobile Association has excellent District Maps that are free to members.

Otherwise several companies produce a variety of maps and road atlas'. Try KiwiMaps or Wise's 2 maps per island series. Both are 500,000:1 and quite reasonably priced. Another option is to use a road atlas, of which all the above companies produce them. Topomaps produce a variety of scales but are comparatively quite expensive.

**BOOKS:** Those people with lots of cash or needing extra ballast have a choice of several general NZ guide books. Popular ones are Lonely Planet's "New Zealand", "Let's Go" and Penguin's "NZ Rough Guide".

Other cycle touring guide books include "NZ by Bike" by Bruce Ringer and "Cycling NZ" by Lonely Planet. Sadly the latter failed to mention this book, even though it was extensively used by their researchers, one of whom also embarked on a little industrial espionage against my one-man operation. Mountain bikers are well served with "Classic NZ Mountain Bike Rides" by Kennet Brothers, specialising in off-road trips.

**SUGGESTED ITINERARY:** North Island touring is well suited for doing smaller circuits, due to the far-flung attractions and highway network. Allowing six months for a good look round is not out-of-order. New Zealand is a relatively small country but there's lots to see. The routes described try to follow prevailing winds, but this is not a tailwind only guarantee!

A recommended grande tour route would be Auckland - Coromandel Peninsula - Rotorua - East Cape - Napier - Route 52 - Wellington. After returning from the South Island bus to Wanganui - Whanganui River Road - National Park and Taupo. Cut across country through Pureora to Te Kuiti and Waitomo Caves. Return to Auckland via Kawhia and Raglan Harbours on SH22. Finish off

with a tour of Northland. That just leaves Lake Waikaremoana, Taranaki and Old Napier - Taihape Road. Next time perhaps or a side trip?

**OTHER:** The North Island is generally more hilly than the South Island, indeed the title for this book was almost "Highways to Heaven"!

So with this in mind it is suggested novices or unfit cyclists should begin their journey on the South Island and start with short daily distances. The routes described try to follow the prevailing wind but this is not a tailwind only guarantee! The less touristified places can be very rewarding places to visit.

Due to the removal of import duties over the last 10 years car prices have plummeted. As a result there has been a considerable increase in traffic volumes but not a similar increase in spending on road maintenance. This means that while NZ is still a Pedallers' Paradise, in some areas it isn't as good as it was and one should take care with which route to use. A mirror is now a useful piece of equipment.

Suggestions from users for cost effective improvements will be appreciated. Things change, please let us know if they do, as with any deliberate mistakes that you find. All routes described in the guide have been travelled by the author, although not all by bicycle. Yet. The author has tried to be humorous, so if something seems odd, that is probably it! Cyclists heading in the opposite direction to the guide will need to read back-to-front, or possibly ride backwards. A Pedallers' Paradise for the South Island is also available. Cycling is not permitted in national parks and on most motorways. Due to the flawed decision making process, cycle helmets are compulsory. Happy pedalling!

**SPECIAL NOTE:** The finger prints on the back cover are your proof this hand-made work of art and reference is the genuine article! They have nothing to do with the wonderful, hard working salesperson's grubby fingers! It is recommended you complain if there are no fingerprints!

# NORTH

**HIGHLIGHTS** (not in any order of preference)

Auckalnd City & Regional Parks
Bay of Islands Maritime Park
Coromandel Peninsula
Hokianga Habour
Cape Reinga & Ninety Mile Beach

Waipu, Poor Knights' & Bream Bay
Matakohe Kauri Museum
Waipoua Forest & Kauri Coast
Haruaki Gulf Maritime Park
Mangonui/Whangaroa Habour Area

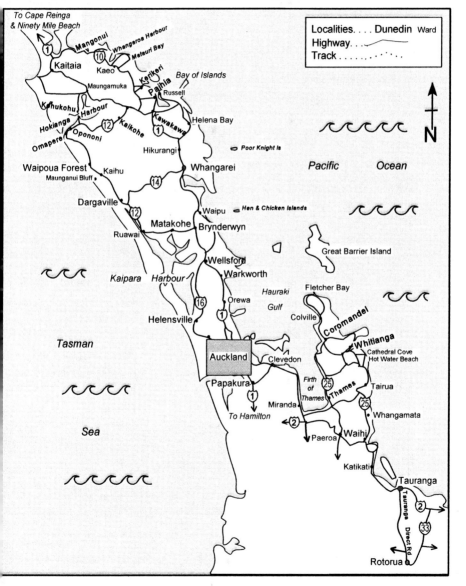

Localities. . . . . Dunedin Ward
Highway. . . .
Track . . . . . . . . . .

To Cape Reinga & Ninety Mile Beach

Mangonui
Whangaroa Harbour
Matauri Bay
① ⑩
Kaitaia
Kaeo
Kerikeri
Paihia
Bay of Islands
Maungamuka
Russell
Kohukohu
Hokianga Harbour
Kaikohe ⑫ Kawakawa ①
Helena Bay
Omapere
Opononi
Hikurangi
Poor Knight Is
Waipoua Forest
Maunganui Bluff
Kaihu
Whangarei
Pacific Ocean
⑭
Dargaville
Hen & Chicken Islands
⑫
Matakohe
Waipu
Ruawai
Brynderwyn
N
Kaipara Harbour
Wellsford
Warkworth
Great Barrier Island
⑯
Orewa
Hauraki Gulf
Fletcher Bay
Helensville
Colville
Coromandel
Tasman
①
Whitianga
Cathedral Cove
Hot Water Beach
Auckland
Clevedon
Papakura
Firth of Thames
⑤ Thames
Tairua
①
Miranda
⑤
Whangamata
Sea
To Hamilton
②
Paeroa
Waihi
Katikati
Tauranga
② Tauranga Direct Rd
㉝
Rotorua

# 1. AUCKLAND.

**DIRECTIONS:** Due to heavy traffic and size of Auckland, it is recommended when possible to take public transport. Frequent shuttle buses operate between the Airport and most central locations, some do not charge for bikes. If travelling to/from the south, suburban trains run between the central city and Papakura. If travelling to/from the north through Helensville, trains run between the central city and Waitakere. To go directly between Waitakere and Papakura either change at Newmarket or new Britomart Transport Interchange (this has replaced Central Station). Trains run Monday to Saturday until 6 or 7 pm. Bikes now cost $1 on the suburban rail network and permitted on trains if they are not busy. The run-down network is being slowly upgraded. See www.rideline.co.nz for detals.

   Those who cycle all the way can expect to encounter heavy traffic. All routes have moderate rolling terrain for much of their length with occasional longer and steeper bits. Cyclists are prohibited on motorways except between the top of Bombay Hill and the SH 1/SH 2 intersection and on parts of the Western Motorway SH 16. The city is developing a network of cycle routes throughout greater Auckland and there is a useful ARC city cycle map available.

**NORTH: Via HELENSVILLE** on SH 16. Go up Queen St from the visitor centre at Aotea Square going right at the T Junction onto Newton Road. There is a new cycle path all the way to Lincoln Rd but you'll need the ARC cycle map to use this route as signage may be a problem. Go right on Triangle Rd and right again onto Don Buck Rd. Go left at T junction onto SH 16, becomes flatter before Kumeu. See Page 11 for onward travel.

   **Via NORTH SHORE** on EAST COAST ROAD. The Harbour Bridge is prohibited to cyclists so take the ferry to Devonport from bottom of Queen St. Head north through Takapuna, join East Coast Road at Pupuke Golf Course and go all the way to Silverdale, where it joins SH 1. The northern motorway is being extended, hopefully making the East Coast Bays route less congested, but no less hilly!! See Section 2a alternative (Page 12) for onward travel but it is not recommended for sane cyclists!

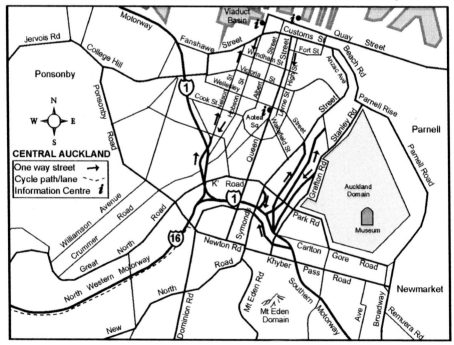

**SOUTH: To COROMANDEL.** Go east (right) along Quay St to Tamaki Drive and follow the 50km cycle route that skirts Waitemata Harbour to Panmure (a special cycle map should be available in Auckland). After crossing Panmure Bridge go through Pakuranga (last supermarket). Pass through the village of Whitford going to Clevedon. See pages 20 - 21 for onward travel.

**To HAMILTON.** Going from the visitor centre at Aotea Square use Wakefield St, Symonds St, and Khyber Pass Rd to get to Newmarket, then go right and join Great South Road. It is quite hilly and suburbs most of the way to Papakura. See pages 68 - 73 for onward travel.

**AIRPORT: To CITY.** Take George Bolt Drive (State Highway 20a) then go left (west) at the traffic lights onto Kirkbride Rd. This becomes Wallace, then Church Road as it swings east, go left at Coronation Rd junction and down to Manukau Harbour. Take the cycle/foot path on the side of the motorway bridge. The old bridge nearby is also useable.

After crossing the harbour, go right under the motorway and join Onehunga Mall. Go through the shopping precinct, left onto Mt Smart Road, through Royal Oak roundabout, onto Mt Albert Road. After 1 mile go right at Three Kings Park onto Mt Eden Road, then Symonds St and left into Wakefield St. Queen St is at the bottom with Aotea Square and main information centre directly opposite. It is possible to use the Coast to Coast track through some of the parks between Royal Oak and central Auckland.

**Going SOUTH.** On leaving Auckland Airport take Tom Pearce Drive which soon becomes Puhinui Road. Stay on this road passing through Puhinui and going all the way to Manukau City. Turn right onto Great South Road. Alternatively, to avoid much of the heavy Auckland traffic, at Puhinui station take a suburban train south to Papakura. See Page 20 for travel to Coromandel. See pages 68 to 73 for travel west to New Plymouth.

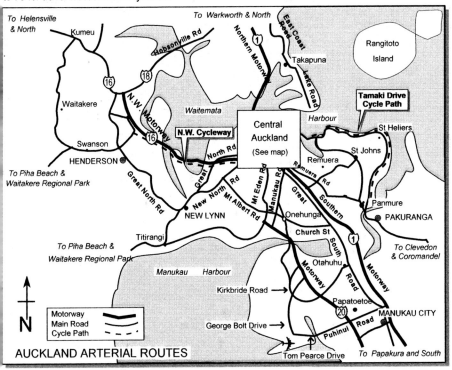

AUCKLAND ARTERIAL ROUTES

# SERVICES: AUCKLAND: Altitude 5-190m, population:1.3 million (approx) ☎ toll call prefix is 09.

Visitor Information Centres: (*i*) 1) Cnr Federal and Victoria Sts ☎ 363 1783.
2) The Viaduct, Cnr Quay & Hobson St.   3) DoC/Regional Parks, Ferry Building, Quay St.
4) Domestic & International Terminals, Auckland Airport.
Food: Many of all types of outlets all over the place.
Accommodation: Motor camp 5 (All suburban); hostel (bkpr 15, YHA 2); motel multitudes; hotel many.
Transport: Trains to/from Wellington stop operating at the end of September. Buses and shuttles to/from just about everywhere.
Bicycle Shops: There are bicycle shops in most suburbs of which below is a sample.
NEWMARKET: * Bike Barn, 50 Remuera Road ☎ 524 5621.
MANUREWA: Dr. Bike, 188 Great South Road, ☎ 266 4837.
GRAFTON: Penny Farthing, Cnr Symonds St & Khyber Pass Rd ☎ 379 2524.
TAKAPUNA: *Hedgehog Cycles, 74 Barrys Pt Rd ☎ 489 6559.
MANUKAU: *Cycle City, 45 Cavendish Rd ☎ 262 1043.
NEW LYNN: Bike Barn, 3119 Great North Road ☎ 827 6951.
HENDERSON: West City Cycles, Edsel St ☎ 383 7693.
Note: Some of these cycle shops also have long term rentals and buy-back schemes.
Auckland Airport has bike stands to assist with the assembly of bikes.

# ATTRACTIONS: Auckland is New Zealand's biggest city with 1.3 million people. The central area

of Auckland spreads across the narrow Tamaki Isthmus between Waitemata and Manukau Harbours. 14 extinct volcanic cones dot the area with over 60 eruption points in greater Auckland. At various times prior to 1840 most have had pa (fortified villages) on their summits.

With a third of New Zealand's population, Auckland has become the main centre for almost everything, especially industrial, commercial and sometimes cultural type activities. It is called the City of Sails and the America's Cup was successfully defended here at the beginning of the new century.

The city has numerous parks, gardens and domains. Some of the better known ones are: Auckland Domain, Mt Eden Mt Albert and Cornwall Park including One Tree Hill (No Tree Hill may now be a better name since the tree was attacked by a chain saw wielding person). Mt Victoria & North Head are on the North Shore. Many incorporate the distinctive volcanic cones and have panoramic views that make the usual steep climb worthwhile. There is also a large network of regional parks spread throughout the greater Auckland area and a comprehensive pamphlet available outlining them.

Some are ideal for exploring and tuning-up the body and bike for longer trips. A coast to coast walk that link the two harbours and a 50 km cycle route around the isthmus have been developed. Both include some of the above features with maps available of the routes.

Rangitoto Island, probably Auckland's most recognisable landmark, is part of the Hauraki Gulf Maritime Park and was the last volcano to become extinct 750 years ago. Regular ferry services around the gulf allow visits to this and other islands, such as Waiheke and Great Barrier.

The city has become culturally diverse in recent years due to a large influx of migrants. Here is the world's largest Polynesian population with increasing numbers from Asia. For shopping expeditions to overload the bike, try Queen Street, Victoria Markets and the suburbs of Parnell, Newmarket, Ponsonby and Devonport. These places also have trendy cafés, bars and nightlife.

As expected there are plenty of manufactured activities for those whose internal and external organs are in need stimulation. Activities includes all kinds of watery sports, jumping off various structures with and without various attachments to various parts of the anatomy.

Try the orgasmic experience of avoiding Auckland's large number of crazed car drivers. The more sedate activities include Kelly Tarlton's Antarctic Encounter & Underwater World, a Maritime Museum, Auckland Museum, MOTAT, Art Gallery, Zoo & various harbour cruises.

# 2. AUCKLAND - BRYNDERWYN - WAIPOUA - KAITAIA.

## ROUTE:

|  | SH 16/12/10 | SH 1 |
|---|---|---|
| 2a) AUCKLAND - BRYNDERWYN | 147 km | 112 km |
| 2b) BRYNDERWYN - WAIPOUA | 125 km | |
| 2c) WAIPOUA - KAITAIA | 123 km | |
| Total | 395 km | |

**ALTERNATIVE** 2a) AUCKLAND - WELLSFORD. The busy, very hilly & sometimes dangerous SH 1 or longer, quiet & hilly SH 16 via Helensville. Both routes meet at Wellsford.
  2b) DARGAVILLE - KAIHU on SH 12 or Ocean Beach.
  2c) HOKIANGA HARBOUR - KAITAIA on SH 1 or via the quiet Broadwood route.
**LINK ROAD** 2b) i DARGAVILLE - MAUNGATAPERE - WHANGAREI on SH 14.
  2c) i HOKIANGA - KAIKOHE - KAWAKAWA on SH 12.
**SIDE TRIP** 2a) WAITAKERE RANGES MEMORIAL PARK & West Coast.
  2a alt) i SILVERDALE - WHANGAPARAOA PENINSULA.
    ii WARKWORTH - MAHURANGI & TAWHARANUI PENINSULAS.
  2c) KAITAIA - CAPE REINGA on SH 1.

## 2a. AUCKLAND - HELENSVILLE - BRYNDERWYN.  147km

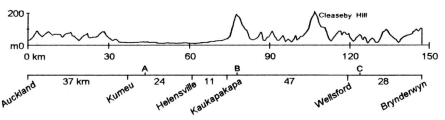

**SERVICES: AUCKLAND:** See pages 8 - 10. The direct route from Auckland to Kumeu is 37 km.
**WAITAKAERE:** Store. Train to/from Auckland. Through Waitakere is a little longer.
**KUMEU:** Alt 30m, store, takeaways. **A) WAIMAUKU:** Tearooms/store.
**PARAKAI:** Store, motor camp, motel 2, hot springs. 2 km off SH 16, 1 km before . . .
**HELENSVILLE:** Alt 10m, pop 1400. Food: All types of outlets. Accom: Bkpr hostel; hotel.
**KAUKAPAKAPA:** Alt 20m, pop 600. Store, hotel.
**B) KAIPARA LOOKOUT:** Alt 180m, picnic area.
**WELLSFORD:** Alt 80m, pop 1700. Food: All types of outlets except supermarket.
Accom: Motel 2; hotel. Transport: Buses to/from Auckland & Bay of Islands.
**C) TE HANA:** Alt 15m, store, takeaways. **KAIWAKA:** Alt 20m, Tearooms, pub, motel.
**BRYNDERWYN:** Alt 110m. Tearooms, motel.

**GRADIENTS:** If cycling between Auckland and Northland this is the recommended route for those who prefer quiet highways. There are no services between Kaukapakapa and Wellsford.

Leave Waitakere and head north on Waitakere Road to Kumeu. Fairly easy gradients between Kumeu and Helensville then undulates from Helensville to 1 km beyond Kaukapakapa. There starts a 2½ km climb to 210m, followed by a 4 km variable descent past Kaipara lookout. Thereafter undulates and rolls along the eastern perimeter of the Kaipara Harbour with occasional longer and steeper hills, particularly around Gorit, a 5 km climb after Tauhoa to leave the harbour over Cleaseby Hill (210m) and down in 3 km, with a quite steep climb after Hoteo North. Gradients then ease to general rolling country for the rest of the way to Wellsford & Brynderwyn.

**ATTRACTIONS:** Out west on a side trip are the Waitakere Ranges and west coast, see options below. Like many of the towns around Auckland and farther north, Helensville was established last century to cater to the needs of the timber industry and has since become a rural service centre. In recent years many vineyards have been established throughout the region. Helensville is at the southern end of the inner Kaipara Harbour, nearby at Parakai are hot springs and further up the south arm is Shelly Beach. Kaipara is NZ's biggest harbour with a shoreline of over 3,000 km, although not very deep. Beyond Wellsford the Brynderwyn Hills have a few walking tracks and offer access to Waipu, Waipu Gorge, Waipu Cove & Waipu caves. Pass through mostly rolling farm country.

**OPTIONS:** SIDE TRIP AUCKLAND - WAITAKERE RANGES MEMORIAL PARK & west coast beaches offer opportunities to explore remote rugged areas close to Auckland. Some steep hills and narrow roads with sometimes heavy traffic. Access through Henderson or Titirangi. There is a comprehensive pamphlet available outlining all the Regional Parks. Up to date information is available from Auckland visitor centre or ARATAKI: *i:* Scenic Dr ☎ 09 817 7134.
PIHA BEACH: motor camp (no cabins) dairy/takeaways. KAREKARE: informal camping (toilets). KAREMATURA VALLEY: informal camping (toilets). Further north from Waimauku is access to MURAWAI BEACH (motor camp, no cabins; motel), on another side trip to another of Auckland's Regional Parks and is popular amongst surfers and gannets.

## 2a ALTERNATIVE. AUCKLAND - WARKWORTH - BRYNDERWYN. 112km

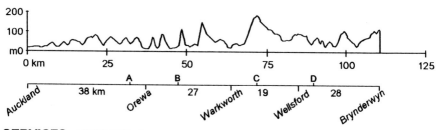

**SERVICES:** AUCKLAND: See pages 8 - 10.
**A) SILVERDALE:** Alt 20m, pop 450. Store, takeaways, motor camp (at Stillwater).
**OREWA:** Pop 5700. Food: All types of outlets. Accom: motor camp 3, bkpr hostel 2, motel 9.
**B) WAIWERA:** Pop 500, store, takeaways, tearooms, motor camp, motel, hotel 2.
**WARKWORTH:** Alt 20m, pop 2000. *i:* 1 Baxter St ☎ 09 425 9081.
Food: All types of outlets. Accom: Motor camp, bkpr hostel, motel 3, hotel.
**C) DOME:** Motor camp, tearooms. **SUNNYBROOK:** Scenic reserve, picnic area.

**WELLSFORD:** Alt 80m, pop 1700. Food: All types of outlets except supermarket. Accom: Motel 2; hotel. Transport: Buses to/from Auckland & Bay of Islands.
**D) TE HANA:** Alt 15m, store, takeaways. **KAIWAKA:** Alt 20m, Tearooms, pub, motel.
**BRYNDERWYN:** Alt 110m, tearooms, motel.

**GRADIENTS:** Too many hills, too much, too fast traffic with too many bends on too narrow roads. It is recommended that novice, unfit or sane cyclists avoid SH 1 between Auckland and Wellsford.

**ATTRACTIONS:** After leaving the suburbs of Auckland behind arrive at Silverdale, the gateway to Whangaparaoa Peninsula (see options below); then Orewa, Hatfield's Beach & Waiwera, all of the Hibiscus Coast and well developed holiday resorts popular with Aucklanders in the summer holidays.
Waiwera has added attractions of thermal pools and nearby Wenderholm Regional Park is considered the most beautiful of all Auckland's regional parks. After the Hibiscus Coast comes the Kowhai Coast around Warkworth and access to Mahurangi & Tawharanui Peninsulas (see options below). Going north pass Dome Valley and Sunnybrook Scenic Reserves. After Wellsford is the Brynderwyn Hills.

**OPTIONS:** SIDE TRIP i SILVERDALE - WHANGAPARAOA PENINSULA & Shakespear Regional Park. Lots of fine views and beaches in this farm park. A popular holiday destination for Aucklanders.
SIDE TRIP ii WARKWORTH - MAHURANGI & TAWHARANUI PENINSULAS. This area is known as the Kowhai Coast. It is a popular summer holiday destination.
Mahurangi Peninsula has several pretty beaches for relaxing on. Snells Beach, Algies Beach and Martins Bay are some of the better known localities. A ferry departs from Sandspit for nearby Kawau Island with its elegant Mansion House, part of the Hauraki Gulf Maritime Park.
Further north and an extension of the same outstanding coastal scenery are Matakana, Omaha, Leigh and Pakiri with Tawharanui Regional Park & Goat Island Marine Reserve.

## 2b. BRYNDERWYN - DARGAVILLE - WAIPOUA FOREST. 125km

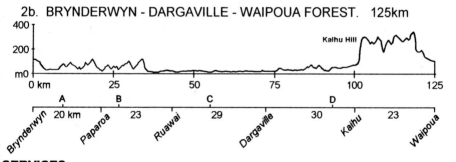

**SERVICES: BRYNDERWYN:** Alt 110m. Tearooms, motel.
**A) MAUNGATUROTO:** Alt 60m, pop 900. Store, takeaways, pub.
**PAPAROA:** Alt 40m, pop 500. Store, takeaways, pub, bkpr hostel/guest house.
**B) MATAKOHE:** Alt 40m *i:* Kauri Museum, Church Rd. ☎ 09 431 6969. Tearooms, motor camp.
**RUAWAI:** Alt 5m, pop 600. Store, takeaways, bkpr hostel, hotel. **C) TOKATOKA:** hotel.
**DARGAVILLE:** Alt 5m, pop 5000. *i:* Normanby St ☎ 09 439 8360. Food: All types of outlets.
Accom: Motor camp 2; bkpr hostel; motel 5; hotel 3. Transport: Shuttle from Bay of Islands to Auckland.
**D) KAI IWI LAKES:** 11 km off SH 12. Domain camping (toilet, water, table).
**KAIHU:** Alt 70m, pop 200. Store, pub, farm hostel, motor camp.
**WAIPOUA FOREST:** Alt 100m. *i:* DoC, ☎ 09 439 0605 Motor camp incl cabins (1½ km off SH 12).

**GRADIENTS:** Predominantly rolling country from Brynderwyn with some longer, steeper bits. Ends with a quite steep 1 km descent. Flat for the last 9 km to Ruawai, continuing the same to Dargaville and 3 km beyond, then undulates and rolls to Kaihu with nothing too serious. That comes after Kaihu tavern. Starting with a steep 3 km climb and followed by many ups and downs, before a 4 km steep descent from Katui (345m) easing for the last 1½ km to Waipoua Forest HQ turn off.

**ATTRACTIONS:** Matakohe Kauri Museum is a definite must see, allow several hours to take it all in. The museum records the history of this remarkable conifer tree that once covered much of northern New Zealand. In effect it is another testament to man's greed that we can, in a few years, almost completely destroy forests that have been here for millions. Happily efforts are being made to right the wrongs of the past.

There are several side trips to the northern reaches of the Kaipara Harbour. Paparoa to Pahi; Matakohe to Tinopai (Domain camping); and Dargaville to Pouto & North Head. Ruawai claims to be kumara (sweet potato) capital, and Tokatoka is watched over by the distinctive Tokatoka Hill. Dargaville, the principal town of the region has a wild west feel to it, the mast from Greenpeace's Rainbow Warrior is on display at the museum.

The region between Kaipara and Hokianga is known as the Kauri Coast. At over 100 km in length, Ocean Beach is New Zealand's longest unbroken stretch of sand, see Options below. At the Kaihu saw mill see the giant logs of swamp kauri, some having lain there many thousands of years (in the swamp, not the saw mill). Around Kaihu are several interesting natural features: Taharoa Domain & Kai Iwi Lakes, clear and deep with no known in or out-let; Maunganui Bluff rising almost vertical from the sea for 460m; Trounson Kauri Park and Waipoua Forest, have the largest remnants of mature kauri forest.

**OPTIONS: ALTERNATIVE** DARGAVILLE - KAIHU. Along Ocean Beach at low tide, several streams to cross, wash the bike with fresh water afterwards. Main access points are from BAYLYS BEACH (Store, motor camp), OMAMARI, KAI IWI LAKES Recreational Reserve (domain camping) and ARANGA BEACH (adjacent Maunganui Bluff).

**LINK ROAD** DARGAVILLE - MAUNGATAPERE - WHANGAREI on SH 14. Distance: 58 km. SH 14 undulates and rolls its way to Whangarei. DARGAVILLE: See above. TANGITERORIA: pub. MAUNGATAPERE: takeaways. WHANGAREI: See page 18.

## 2c. WAIPOUA FOREST - HOKIANGA HARBOUR - KAITAIA.   123km

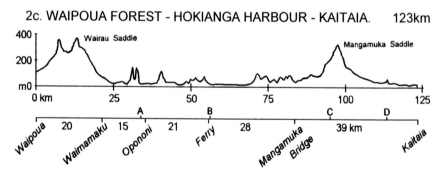

**SERVICES:** WAIPOUA FOREST: Alt 100m. DoC motor camp incl cabins (1½ km off SH 12).
**WAIMAMAKU:** Alt 40m, pop 150. Store, pub.
**A) OMAPERE:** pop 400. *i:* Museum, SH 12 ☎ 09 405 8869. Store, tearooms, bkpr hostel, motel, hotel.
**OPONONI:** Alt 5m, pop100. Food: Store, takeaways, tearooms, restaurant.
Accom: Motor camp, bkpr hostel 2, motel, hotel.
**RAWENE:** Alt 5m, pop 400. Store, takeaways, pub, hotel. Ferry to/from . . .
**B) KOHUKOHU:** Alt 5m, pop 150. Store, tearooms, hotel, bkpr hostel (near ferry).
**MANGAMUKA BRIDGE:** Alt 20m, pop 150. Hotel.
**C) MANGAMUKA:** Recreation Res. Alt 80m, Informal camping (toilet, water, table).
**FOREST LOOKOUT:** picnic area. **MANGAMUKA SADDLE:** Alt 380m, picnic area.
**RAETEA FOREST:** Informal camping. **D) PAMAPURIA:** Alt 25m, Store.
**KAITAIA:** Alt 15m, pop 5000. *i:* Jaycee Park, South Road, SH 1 ☎ 09 408 0879.
Food: All types of outlets. Accom: Motor camp (no cabins); hostel (bkpr 1, YHA 1); motel 7; hotel 3.
Transport: Several bus & shuttles to/from Cape Reinga, Bay of Islands & Auckland.
Bicycle Shop: Cycle Sport n Heat Shop, 167 Commerce St ☎ 09 408 0812.

**GRADIENTS:** After Forest HQ two more substantial hills follow, the first having a 7 km gradual climb and the last has a 6 km variable steep descent from Waiau Saddle (387m) to Waimamaku. After Waimamaku are 7 km of easy gradients, then two steep hills before arriving at Omapere on the Hokianga, from where SH 12 undulates alongside the harbour to Opononi. After Opononi head cross country with one quite steep hill to climb. Leave SH 12 to go to Rawene, arriving back at the harbour to take the ferry to Kohukohu.

The first 11 km from the ferry are flat, passing through Kohukohu, then rolls most of the way to Mangamuka Bridge & SH 1. Mostly easy gradients from there to Mangamuka Scenic Reserve, when SH 1 climbs for 5 km, steep and winding in places to Mangamuka Saddle (380m). Down again in similar fashion for 4 km before levelling out at Raetea Reserve and easing to a steady gentle descent with hills gradually falling back. Becomes almost flat to Kaitaia, except for a tiny hill at Pampuria.

**ATTRACTIONS:** Waipoua Forest covers 9000ha and has the largest and oldest known kauri within its boundaries; Tane Mahuta (god of the forest) & Te Matua Ngahere (Lord of the forest), are thought to be up to 2,000 year old. The Four Sisters are amongst several other stands of mature kauri found throughout the park, as well as large areas of regenerating growth comprising of mixed bush.

Going north, Hokianga Harbour is in a picturesque setting with huge sand dunes at the mouth of the harbour and quaint villages like Omapere, Opononi, Rawene & Kohukohu dotting the shoreline. Rich in historic and scenic features, It has the oldest Maori & second oldest European settlements. In recent years it has become popular with arty types and a thriving craft industry(?) exists. Legend has it the famous Maori navigator Kupe returned to Hawaiki from here and is the ancestral home of the Ngapuhi Tribe. Opo the dolphin became famous at Opononi, see archive film in the museum. Going north pass through Mangamuka Scenic Reserve. Kaitaia is the gateway to Cape Reinga & Ninety Mile Beach, (see options below) and is a small bustling town that services the surrounding communities.

**OPTIONS: ALTERNATIVE ii** KOHUKOHU - BROADWOOD - KAITAIA. Distance 76 km.
9 km longer than SH 1 through Mangamuka. Quieter than SH 1 and rolling without the long climb and descent of the Mangamuka Saddle. Mostly flat from Ahipara to Kaitaia. Pass through bush and farm country. Ahipara is at the bottom end of Ninety Mile Beach. BROADWOOD: store, bkpr hostel. HEREKINO: pub. AHIPARA: dairy, takeaways, motor camp, bkpr hostel, motel.

**LINK ROAD i** OPONONI - KAIKOHE - KAWAKAWA on SH 12/1. Distance 88 km, Opononi - Kaikohe 55 km, Kaikohe - Kawakawa 33 km. Some long, gradual climbs and descents with occasional steeper bits. Kaikohe is the largest settlement of this area. Pass near to Ngawha thermal pools, and Lake Omapere, Northland's biggest, formed in the crater of an extinct volcano. At Waimate North is NZ's first mission station and second house. OPONONI: See above.
KAIKOHE: Alt 200m, pop 4000. Food: All types of outlets. Accom: Motel; hotel 2.
NGAWHA: 3 km off SH 12, hot springs, motel (also camping but no kitchen). OHAEAWAI: store, takeaways, hotel. MOEREWA: Store, takeaways, tearooms, hotel. KAWAKAWA: See page 18.

**LINK ROAD ii** MANGAMUKA BRIDGE - KAWAKAWA on SH 1. Distance 62 km. Steep hills in places. Access to Omahuta & Puketi Forests from several places.
MANGAMUKA BRIDGE: See above. UMAWERA: Shop/tearooms in petrol station.
FOREST POOLS: 2 km off SH 1, DoC camping (toilet, water). OKAIHAU: Alt 150m, pop 300. Store, takeaways, hotel. OHAEAWAI: Alt 150m, pop 450. Store, takeaways, hotel.
MOEREWA: Store, takeaways, tearooms, hotel. KAWAKAWA: See page 18.

**SIDE TRIP i** KAITAIA - CAPE REINGA. Distance 115 km (one way) on SH 1.
Where the Tasman Sea and Pacific Ocean meet but not the most northerly point in NZ, the nearby North Cape has that honour. Tradition has it that the souls of the dead gather here for a final rest before making the long journey home to the land of their ancestors.
WAIPAPAKAURI: Pub. WAIPAPAKAURI BEACH: Motor camp (5km off SH1).
PUKENUI: Store, takeaways, motor camp, bkpr hostel/motel. HOUHORA: Motel.
NGATAKI: Bkpr hostel at Henderson Bay (5 km off SH 1) & DoC camping (toilet, water, table, cold shower, mosquitoes) at Rawara Beach, a few km N. TE KAO: Store.
WAITAKI LANDING: Dairy/tearooms/motor camp/pub, bkpr hostel.
TE PAKI RESERVE: DoC camping (toilet, water, table, cold shower, mosquitoes) at Spirit's & Tapotupotu Bays. The last 21 km from Waitaki Landing are gravel. As with all trips to remote locations, obtain up-to-date information before proceeding. Travel along Ninety Mile Beach (actually only 56 miles long) is possible at low tide. Afterwards use  fresh water to wash the salt off your bike.

# 3. KAITAIA - PAIHIA - BRYNDERWYN - AUCKLAND.

**ROUTE:**

| | SH 10/1/16 | SH 1 |
|---|---|---|
| 3a) KAITAIA - PAIHIA | 125 km * | |
| 3b) PAIHIA - BRYNDERWYN | 126 km ** | |
| 3c) BRYNDERWYN - AUCKLAND | <u>147 km</u> *** | 112 km |
| Total: | 398 km | |

*Includes 5 km to visit Kerikeri.  **Includes 3 km to visit Waipu.  ***See pages 11/12.

**ALTERNATIVE** 3a) WHANGAROA - KERIKERI on SH 10 or hilly gravel Matauri Bay Road.
   3b) i RUSSELL - WHAKAPARA. on SH 1 or a sometimes rough gravel road via Whangaruru.
      ii WAIPU - WELLSFORD on SH 1 or through scenic Mangawhai.
**SIDE TRIP** 3a)  i To KARIKARI PENINSULA (Doubtless Bay). ii To PUKETI FOREST
**LINK ROAD** 3b) i KAWAKAWA - MANGAMUKA BRIDGE on SH 1. See this page above.
   ii KAWAKAWA - KAIKOHE - OPONONI on SH 12. See  this page above.
   iii WHANGAREI - DARGAVILLE on SH 14, see page 14.

## 3a. KAITAIA - MANGONUI - PAIHIA (and Russell). 124km

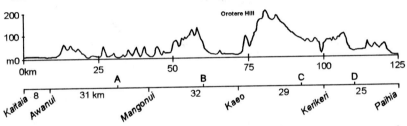

**SERVICES: KAITAIA:** See previous section. **AWANUI:** Store, takeaways, tearooms, pub, motel.
**A) TAIPA:** Alt 5m, pop 300. Dairy, takeaways, pub, motel 3.
**CABLE BAY:** Store/tearooms, motel. **COOPER'S BEACH:** Tearooms, takeaway, store, motel 3.
**MANGONUI:** (1 km off SH 10), pop 550. Store, tearooms, restaurant, bkpr hostel, motel 3, hotel.
**HIHI BEACH:** (6km off SH 10) motor camp. **B) KAHOE:** Bkpr hostel.
**WHANGAROA:** (6 km off SH 10), pop 260. Food: Store, restaurant. Accom: motor camp (1km before
the village); bkpr hostel; motel 2; hotel. **KAEO:** Alt 15m, pop 400. Store, tearooms, takeaways, pub.
**OROTERE HILL:** Alt 200m, picnic area. **C) WAIPAPA:** Alt 80, pop 200, dairy, tearooms.
**KERIKERI:** Altitude 50m, pop 2000. Food: All types of outlets. Accom: Motor camp 2; hostel (Bkpr 2,
YHA 1); motel 8; hotel. Bicycle Shop: Keri Cycles, Cobham Rd, ☎ 09 407 7040.
**D) PUKETONA:** (junction SH 1 & Paihia Road) Alt 50m, tearooms/takeaways, motel.
**HARURU FALLS:** Dairy, motor camp 2, hotel, motel 2. **WAITANGI:** Motor camp, hotel.
**PAIHIA:** Altitude 5m, population 2000. *i:* Maritime Building, Marsden Road ☎ 09 402 7345.
Food: All types of outlets except supermarket. Accom: Motor Camp; bkpr hostel 7; motel lots; hotel 6.
Transport: Ferry to/from Russell. Bus to/from Auckland, Cape Reinga & West Coast.
**RUSSELL:** Alt 5m, pop 1000. *i:* The Strand ☎ 09 403 9020. Food: All types of outlets except
supermarket. Accom: Motor camp 2; bkpr hostel 2; motel 6; hotel 2.

**GRADIENTS:** Flat for the first 10 km from Kaitaia as SH 10 heads across Awanui Plains, then
alternates between sometimes steep, rolling country and gentle undulations. Becomes increasingly hilly
through Doubtless Bay to Mangonui. After Mangonui is a short respite then back into the hills again,
ending with a long gradual descent to Whangaroa Harbour.
    Then mostly flat, broken by an occasional short hill as SH 10 skirts the harbour's southern perimeter.
Flattish passing through Kaeo, before one small hill and a long 3-4 km variable climb up Orotere Hill
(200m). Then rolls and undulates, with a final, long gradual descent to Waipapa.
    The detour from Waipapa to Kerikeri and back to SH 10 is easy except for a short steep drop in and
climb out of Kerikeri Basin. After Waipapa SH 10 undulates, with steep rolls, for 5 km to Kerikeri's
southern entrance, then easy gradients until a long steep descent through Puketona Scenic Reserve.
Flat for the last 2 km to Puketona, then mostly rolling to Paihia.

**ATTRACTIONS:** Karikari Peninsula, Taipa, Cable Bay, Cooper's Beach and Mangonui are all
popular summer holiday resorts on Doubtless Bay, also called the Crystal Coast. Totara North &
Whangaroa are on the picturesque Whangaroa Harbour with St Paul's Rock (a volcanic plug) watching
over things and looking ready for a third encounter. In 1809 the sailing ship *Boyd* was attacked and
plundered with most her crew becoming a gourmet meal of the local tribe. Nearby is Matauri Bay and
Cavalli Islands has the sunken wrecks of the Rainbow Warrior and a couple of warships, which is now
popular for diving expeditions. Catch a glimpse of rare buffalo with an aqua-lungs. Puketi State Forest
is on a side trip inland, containing abundant native flora and fauna.

The climate and soil combine to make Kerikeri an important horticultural region, kiwifruit and citrus fruits are specialities. Kerikeri Basin has Kemp House and Stone Store are New Zealand's oldest European wooden and stone buildings respectively. The adjacent Rewa's Village is a reconstructed pre-European Maori village and nearby are Rainbow Falls. Pass Haruru Falls on the way to Paihia.

Paihia, Russell, Waitangi, Waimate North, Kerikeri and Opua are the main localities of the Bay of Islands Maritime & Historic Park, an extremely popular holiday destination. In spite of the tourism boom, the Bay of Islands remain a beautiful place to visit. Some of NZ's first European settlements were established in the area. An important part of New Zealand history occurred here on 6th Feb 1840 when the Treaty of Waitangi was signed in what is now the Waitangi National Reserve.

Okiato or Old Russell became the first capital but it was later moved to Auckland and then Wellington, but that is another story. Amongst the attractions are, once more, plenty of aquatic type activities, i.e. sea kayaking, game fishing, diving, dolphin swimming and cream & sail boat cruises. Also there are a few nature walks, a shipwreck museum and a steam train to Kawakawa that takes bikes.

**OPTIONS: ALTERNATIVE** WHANGAROA HARBOUR - KERIKERI. About 30 km longer than SH 10. Hilly, partly gravel, often steep, narrow and winding road, reaching 200m in places, passing near to TAURANGA BAY (motor camp, motel) and MATAURI BAY (motor camp, hotel). Rejoins SH 10 about 9 km SE of Kaeo.

**SIDE TRIP i** To KARIKARI PENINSULA on the outer arm of Doubtless Bay. Yet more in a long line of idyllic beauty spots. KARIKARI BAY (Motor camp). MATAI BAY (DoC camping; toilet, water, table). RANGIPUTA: (Motel 2).

**SIDE TRIP ii** To PUKETI FOREST (DoC hut & camping; toilet, water). Tramping tracks, abundant native flora & fauna including stands of mature kauri. Can be reach from several directions on mostly gravel roads. A place to escape the beach culture for a while.

## 3b. PAIHIA - WHANGAREI - BRYNDERWYN.    126km

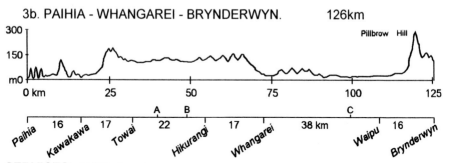

**SERVICES: PAIHIA:** See above.

**KAWAKAWA:** Alt 20m, pop 1700. Food: All types of outlets except supermarket. Accom: Motel; hotel. Bicycle Shop: Turton's Sports & Cycles, Gillies St ☎ 09 404 0681.

**TOWAI:** Alt 115m, tearooms, pub. **A) HUKERENUI:** Alt 110m, pub.

**B) WHAKAPARA:** Dairy/takeaways. **HIKURANGI:** Alt 100m, pop 1300. Store, takeaways, hotel.

**PIANO HILL:** Bkpr hostel. **KAMO:** Dairy, takeaways, motor camp, hotel.

**WHANGAREI:** Alt 10m, pop 45,000. *i:* Tarewa Park, Otaika Rd ☎ 09 438 1079. Food: All types of outlets. Accom: Motor camp 3; hostel (bkpr 3, YHA 1); motel many; hotel 3. Bicycle Shop: *Motocat Cyclery, 70 James St ☎ 09 438 1168. *Hedgehog Bikes, 29 Vine St ☎ 09 438 2521. Transport: Bus & shuttle to/from Kaitaia, Bay of Islands & Auckland.

**C) RUAKAKA:** 1 km off SH 1, pop 1000. Store, takeaways, restaurant, pub. Motor camp 2; motel 3.

**URETITI BEACH:** Alt 5m, DoC camping adjacent SH1 (toilet, water, table, cold shower).

**WAIPU:** 1½ km off SH 1, alt 20m, pop 600. Store, dairy/tearooms, pub, motor camp, bkpr hostel (at beach 4 km along Waipu Cove Road), motel. **PILBROW HILL:** Alt 300m, Tearooms, picnic area. **BRYNDERWYN:** Alt 110m, tearooms, motel.

**GRADIENTS:** There are several quite long, steep hills between Paihia and Kawakawa, then becomes flat on joining SH 1. After 7 km there is a 3 km long variable climb to 180m and a rolling 5 km descent. Predominantly undulating through Towai and Hukerenui, becoming gentle around Whakapara. Rolls begin again at Hikurangi with increasing frequency and height towards Whangarei ending with long gradual descent into the city.

Several kms of moderate rolls takes one out of town, becoming gentle as Ruakaka & Bream Bay nears, then flat to Waipu. After Waipu a gentle climb starts, becoming steeper and twisting for 5 km after Waipu Gorge Road until the top of Pilbrow Hill (300m). Down steep, winding in places for 180m in 2½ km to Piroa Stream, then eases to rolling down, arriving at SH 10/1 junction at Brynderwyn.

**ATTRACTIONS:** Near Kawakawa are Waiomo limestone caves and Ruapekapeka pa, the site of the last battle between Hone Heke's Maoris & British troops in 1846, the victory being less than honourable. Nearby Waimate North has the first inland mission house and second oldest building in New Zealand, which has been restored to its orginal condition. Russell Road through Whangaruru is a usually quieter route to take, see option below.

Whangarei is the biggest city north of Auckland. It is a base from which to explore the Poor Knight's Maritime Reserve, one of the world's best diving locations. Whangarei Falls is a popular beauty spot. Ocean going yachts often use Whangarei as a stopping point. Marsden Point has a oil refinery.

Going south, Bream Bay is between Bream Head and Bream Tail (yes it is true) is a popular holiday area and has several scenic gems, especially around Waipu. Overlooked by the Brynderwyn Hills and adjacent to the Hen & Chicken Islands. Nearby are Uretiti Beach, Waipu Cove, Waipu Caves, and Mangawhai Heads. There are plenty of opportunities for fishing and relaxing type activities.

**OPTIONS: ALTERNATIVE i** RUSSELL - WHANGARURU - WHAKAPARA. Distance: 75 km.
This route is 16 km longer than SH 1, on a scenic, more interesting but often hilly, narrow and winding road going from Russell to Whakapara. Pass several tiny communities and holiday resorts. Elevation gain/loss is sometimes 200m, becomes flatter approaching Whakapara.
RUSSELL: See Section 3a above. WHANGARURU: bkpr farm hostel.
OAKURA BAY: dairy, takeaways, motor camp (1km N), motel/motor camp. WHAKAPARA: See above.
There are several side trips to get to even farther away from it all type places, each with their own special character ie: to Cape Brett, to Bland Bay & Whangaruru North Head, to Mimiwhangata Coastal Park. Or continue south to Whangarei on a complicated network of back roads close to the east coast via WHANANAKI: shop/motor camp, DoC camping (toilet, water). TUTUKAKA: hotel, motel and...

**ALTERNATIVE ii** WAIPU - MANGAWHAI - WELLSFORD. Distance: 47 km.
This route is 10 km longer, has less traffic, is prettier, preferable, and more interesting. Avoids SH 1 traffic and Brynderwyn Hills but has a few hills of its own but with lots of fine views.
WAIPU: Alt 20m, pop 600. Store, dairy/tearooms, pub, motor camp, bkpr hostel (at the beach 4 km along Waipu Cove Road), motel. WAIPU COVE: Dairy/takeaways, motor camp 2, motel 2.
LANGS BEACH: picnic area. MANGAWHAI HEADS: dairy, motor camp 2, bkpr hostel, motel 2.
MANGAWHAI: Alt 10m, pop 400. Store, tearooms, motor camp 2. TE HANA: (SH 1). See page 13.

**3c. BRYNDERWYN - WELLSFORD - AUCKLAND:** See Section 2 (pages 11 &12).

# 4. AUCKLAND - PAEROA - COROMANDEL - ROTORUA.

**ROUTES:**         via Clevedon & Miranda         SH 2
4a) AUCKLAND - PAEROA         137 km*
4b) PAEROA - ROTORUA                                         145 km
\* 6 km less if going direct to Thames (for Coromandel Peninsula).

| **COROMANDEL PENINSULA** | SH 25 |
|---|---|
| 4a i THAMES - WHITIANGA | 101 km |
| 4a ii WHITIANGA - WAIHI | 108 km |
| Total | 209 km |

**ALTERNATIVE** 4ai) i COROMANDEL - WHITIANGA on 309 Road or SH 25 (Page 22).
        ii WHITIANGA - WHENUAKITE on SH 25 or via Hahei and Hot Water Beach (Page 24).
    4b) i WAIHI - WAIHI BEACH - SH 2 (Page 25).
        ii TAURANGA - ROTORUA on Tauranga Direct Rd or SH 33 (Page 24/25).
**SIDE TRIP** 4a) KAUAERANGA FOREST PARK (off SH 25) on a partly gravel track (Page 21).
    4a i) COROMANDEL - COLVILLE - FLETCHER BAY - PORT CHARLES (Page 22).
**LINK ROAD:** 4a) i KOPU - HIKUAI on SH 25a. ii KOPU - PAEROA on SH 26 (Page 21).
    4ai) TAPU - COROGLEN on a gravel road (Page 23).

## 4a. AUCKLAND - MIRANDA - PAEROA (or Thames).          137km

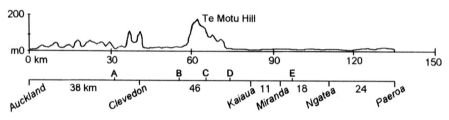

**SERVICES: AUCKLAND:** See Section 1 (page 8-10). **A) WHITFORD:** dairy.
**CLEVEDON:** Alt 15m, pop 700. Tearooms, takeaways, dairy, restaurant, pub.
**B) KAWAKAWA BAY:** Pop 400. Dairy, motel. **C) ORERE PT:** 2 km off highway, motor camp.
**D) WAHARAU:** Regional Park, picnic area (toilets, table, water).
**KAIAUA:** Alt 5m, pop 500. Store, tearooms, takeaways, dairy, motor camp, hotel.
**MIRANDA:** Wildlife trust hostel; motor camp (hot pools included in price).
**E) WAITAKARURU:** Alt 5m, pop 200. Store, pub. From here go to either Paeroa . . .
**NGATEA:** Alt 5m, pop 900. Store, tearooms, restaurant,  motel, hotel.
**PAEROA:** Alt 5m, pop 3800. *i:* Belmont Rd ☎ 07 862 8636. Food: All types of outlets.
Accom: motor camp; motel 3; hotel. Transport: Bus & shuttle to/from Auckland, Coromandel Peninsula
& Tauranga. Bicycle Shop: Paeroa Marine & Cycles, 29 Puke Rd ☎ 07 862 7061.
    Or if going from Waitakaruru direct to Thames and Coromandel Peninsula pass through . . .
**PIPIROA:** tearooms. **KOPU:** Tearooms, pub, restaurant, motel. **THAMES:** See next section (4ai).

**GRADIENTS:** Join Clevedon Road at Papakura station and go on a mostly easy road to Clevedon continuing similar on to Kawakawa Bay. Immediately on departing Kawakawa Bay, a 3 km climb begins, gentle at first, becoming steep and winding to 170m, then down for 1 km through Te Motu Scenic Reserve. On emerging from the bush the highway rolls, tracking down before joining the Firth of Thames at Matingarahi. Mostly flat from there, at Waitakaruru go left to either Paeroa or Thames. Note: To Coromandel Peninsula see next section (4ai). To Tauranga and beyond via SH 2 see page 24. To Rotorua and beyond through Paeroa and Tirau, see page 37-38.

**ATTRACTIONS:** Leave the city behind passing through the small settlements of Whitford, Clevedon and Kawakawa Bay. Travel alongside the Firth of Thames for many miles, passing Tapapakanga & Waharau Regional Parks, Miranda hot springs & bird sanctuary.

Kauaeranga Forest, in the rugged Coromandel Forest Park near Thames offers plenty of tramping possibilities such as Billy Goat Track to the Pinnacles. Plenty of native forest, historical sites and DoC camp sites (toilet, table, water) and huts. The flat Hauraki Plains, once mostly swamp is now fertile farming country. Paeroa, at one time a shipping port, is now many km inland.

**OPTIONS:** **LINK ROAD i** KOPU - HIKUAI on SH 25a. Distance: 29 km.
Starts gentle gradients for 4 km then rolls uphill for 4 km with a last 6 km variable climb to 420m (picnic area). 4 km down, some steep, then 3 long roller coaster type hills before moderating to a gradual down to SH 25/25a junction at Hikuai. Left to Coromandel, right to Whangamata.
   **LINK ROAD ii** KOPU - PAEROA on SH 26. Distance 26 km. SH 26 from Kopu to Paeroa gently rolls and undulates as it travels along the foothills of the Coromandel Range.
KOPU: See above. PURIRI: pub. HIKUTAIA: Store, pub. PAEROA: See above.

## 4a Side Trip i: THAMES - COROMANDEL - WHITIANGA.   100km

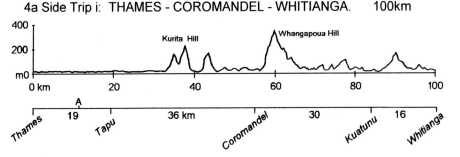

**SERVICES: THAMES:** Pop 6500. *i:* 206 Pollen St ☎ 07 868 7284. Food: All types of outlets. Accom: Motor camp; bkpr hostel; motel 5; hotel 4. Transport: Bus & shuttle to/from Auckland, Tauranga & Coromandel Peninsula. Bicycle Shop: Paki Paki Bike Shop, Goldfields Centre ☎ 07 867 9026.
**TARARU:** Pub, motel. **A) TE PURU:** Pop 500. Dairy, motor camp; motel/restaurant.
**WAIOMU:** Dairy. motor camp; motel 2; hotel. **TE MATA:** Cabins.
**WAIKAWAU:** Picnic area. **RAUMAHANGA BAY:** Motel.
**TAPU:** Alt 5m, pop 400. Store/tearooms, motor camp, hotel. **KURITA HILL:** Alt 205m. Picnic area.
**COROMANDEL:** Alt 10m, pop 1000. *i:* 355 Kapanga Rd ☎ 07 866 8598. Food: All types of outlets except supermarket. Accom: Motor camp 2; bkpr hostel 3; motel 3; hotel.
**WHANGAPOUA:** (5 km off SH 25) motor camp, store/caravans. **MATARANGI:** (3 km off SH 25) dairy.
**KUAOTUNU:** Store, takeaways, motor camp; bkpr hostel. **WHITIANGA:** See next section.

**GRADIENTS:** Mostly flat for 34 km from Thames as SH 25 heads along the coast. Then a steep 200m climb in 2 km, 1 km quite steep down and up 115m in 1½ km to Kerita Hill (206m). A steady quite steep 3 km descent then flat to skirt round Manaia Harbour before climbing again for 1 mile, beginning with a short very steep section, easing near to the top at 160m. Down again, variable steep for 3 km before returning to gentle gradients for the last stretch into Coromandel township.

After leaving Coromandel town, SH 25 climbs steep, winding 3½ km to 370m to the top of Whangapoua Hill (tar-sealing is now finished), then descends steep for 3 km, afterwhich it rolls down. Mostly rolling and undulating with three bigger, steeper hills between Matarangi turnoff and Kuaotunu. Try the interesting Bluff Road instead of SH 25 between Matarangi & Kuaotunu Bays.

After Kuaotunu SH 25 heads inland, going gentle uphill at first but becoming steeper for 2½ km before reaching 140m. Down variable steep for 4 km then undulates to Wharekai, followed by one smallish hill and then flat for the last 3 km into Whitianga.

**ATTRACTIONS:** Thames is the gateway to Coromandel Peninsula, but apart from a side trip the Kauaeranga Valley and a few relics from the gold mining era, it has little to offer, especially considering the attractions beyond. It is hard to believe at one time the population was bigger than Auckland. Travel many miles along the coast, see the converted tram holiday homes, particularly around Tapu. While the west of the peninsula is pretty, the north and east coasts have the spectacular scenery.

Rich in native flora, the peninsula is an important habitat for the pohutakawa, New Zealand's Christmas tree. Tramping opportunities are possible from several access points into Coromandel Forest Park. All around the peninsula opportunities are available for a multitude of activities.

The main points of interest on the remote northern arm of the peninsula are Colville, Fletcher Bay, Port Charles and Mt Moehau. The 309 Road is a shorter pleasant alternative to SH 25 from Coromandel to Whitianga and has several points of interest on it. See the alternative option below. After crossing the dividing range, Whangapoua Harbour is the start of a stream of stunning scenery.

**OPTIONS: ALTERNATIVE** COROMANDEL - WHITIANGA on 309 Road. Distance: 33 km.
After 4 km leave SH 25 and travel on a typical gravel Coromandel road, narrow, winding and corrugated. Rolls uphill for 8 km to 300m followed by varying degrees of downhill for 5 km, then rolling down to rejoin SH 25 followed by a mostly flat 7 km to Whitianga. Muddy when wet.

309 Road has quite a few points of interest along the way. In quick succession pass the access track to the imposing 520m Castle Rock; Chiltern Scenic Reserve; Waiau Falls and Kauri Grove including a set of siamese twins. Around the saddle is Mohutere Scenic Reserve.

**SIDE TRIP** COROMANDEL - COLVILLE - FLETCHER BAY - PORT CHARLES.
All tracks are gravel after Colville. Some flat bits to Fantail Bay then mostly hilly, winding, narrow, with corrugations and occasional fast car. Otherwise brilliant cycling! A circuit can be made by taking the difficult walkway between Fletcher & Stony Bays, that has been widened to take mountain bikes, get up-to-date info before using.

Remote. Lots of tiny bays and inlets to explore. Colville general store is itself a tourist attraction and the last place to get supplies if heading north. Mt Moehau at 890m is Coromandel's highest mountain and it is at the narrowest point on the peninsula. A walking track goes to the top from Stony Bay and Te Hope Stream. SHELLY BEACH: Motor camp, motel. PAPA AROHA BAY: Motor camp/shop, motel. AMODEO BAY: Motor camp, motel. COLVILLE: Store, tearooms, bkpr farm hostel, motel. FANTAIL BAY: DoC camping (toilet, water). FLETCHER BAY: DoC camping (toilet, water); bkpr hostel. STONY BAY: DoC camping (toilet, water). PORT CHARLES: DoC camping (toilet, water).

**LINK ROAD:** TAPU - COROGLEN. 29 km on a gravel road, a lot of it up and a lot of it down. The main attraction is the Square Kauri, about 8 km from Tapu.

## 4a Side Trip ii. WHITIANGA - TAIRUA - WHANGAMATA - WAIHI.   108km

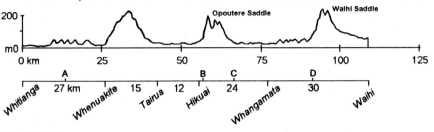

**SERVICES: WHITIANGA:** Alt 5m, pop 2300. *i:* 66 Albert St ☎ 07 866 5555.
Food: All types of outlets. Accom: Motor camp 3; bkpr hostel 2; motel 14; hotel 2.
Transport: Ferry to/from Ferry Landing (for Hahei & Hot Water Beaches). Shuttle from Thames to Whangamata. Bicycle Shop: Bike Man, 16 Coghill St ☎ 07 866 0745.
**A) COROGLEN:** Store, pub. **WHENUAKITE:** Motor camp.
**TAIRUA:** Alt 5m, pop 1200. Food: All types of outlet except supermarket. Accom: Motor camp, bkpr hostel 2, motel 2, hotel. **HIKUAI:** DoC camping (toilet, table, water) 4 km off SH 25 at Broken Hills.
**PAUANUI:** 12 km off SH 25. Store, motel 2, hotel. **B) SH 25/25a JUNCT:** Alt 40m, picnic area.
**C) OPOUTERE:** 4 km off SH 25. Motor camp, YHA hostel.
**WHANGAMATA:** Alt 10m, pop 2000. *i:* Port Rd ☎ 07 865 8340.
Food: All types of outlets. Accom: Motor camp 2; bkpr hostel 2; motel 3; hotel.
Bicycle Shop: *Whangamata Cycles, Port Rd ☎ 07 865 8096.
**D) WHIRITOA:** Alt 10m, dairy/takeaways. **WAIHI:** See next section.

**GRADIENTS:** Flat at first then becomes rolling shortly after 309 Road turn off through Coroglen and for most of the way to Whenuakite. After Whenuakite are easy gradients to Whenuakite Stream, when begins a long wending and sometimes steep ascent to 220m, abating as the top nears. Variably downhill at first, SH 25 becomes steep and winding as it passes the Twin Kauris, eventually gradients diminish to a gentle decline into Tairua.
  The highway heads inland after Tairua, gently undulating as it skirts alongside the harbour to Hikuai. At SH 25/25a junction the road climbs quite steeply to Opoutere Saddle (200m), a shortish but steep descent and climb, then rolls before a variable 3 km downhill, levelling out at Opoutere turn off. Rolls and undulates from there with no serious hills and becoming flat as Whangamata nears. Rolling from Whangamata to beyond Whiritoa until a 4 km quite steep climb to cross Whiritoa/Waihi Saddle (236m). There are 4 km of hairpin bends around the top. The road descends for 1½ km, climbs for 1 km then swoops down variably again for another 5 km. Levels out to almost flat for the last few km to Waihi.

**ATTRACTIONS:** Both navigators extraordinaire, Kupe & Capt Cook visited Mercury Bay, making them amongst the first tourists here, but did they go to the information centre first? Cook came in 1769 to watch the transit of Mercury (hence Mercury Bay). At the same time he declared New Zealand a British Colony. After Whitianga, going through Coroglen is less interesting than the alternative through Hahei and Hot Water Beaches, see options below.

After Mercury Bay & Whitianga the stunning scenery continues going most of the way to Whangamata. Cook's Beach & Flaxmere Bay; Hahei Beach & Cathedral Cove; Hot Water Beach & the hot pools at low tide; Twin Kauris, Tairua & Paku Hill; Hikuai & Broken Hills; Opoutere & Wharekawa Harbour; Whangamata & Wentworth Valley. These are some of the notable places en route. Marine reserves, scenic reserves, historic reserves, wildlife reserves, so much abundant natural beauty. So much lush bush, even in heavy rain it is appealing. Help! Is this sounding like a travelogue? Well, next comes Waihi and the big hole! Note: Coromandel Peninsula is very crowded during summer holidays.

**OPTIONS: ALTERNATIVE** WHITIANGA - HAHEI & HOT WATER BEACHES - WHENUAKITE. Distance 30 km, includes going in/out of Hahei and Hot Water Beaches. Take the small ferry from Whitianga to Ferry Landing, the road rolls and undulates as it travels past tiny bays & inlets. Rejoin SH 25 at Whenuakite. This area has the highest concentration of outstanding natural features on the Peninsula, having amongst others, Cook's Beach, Flaxmere Bay, Hahei Beach, Cathedral Cove, Hot Water Beach. Very busy in summer.
FLAXMILL BAY: Motel 3, cabins. COOKS BEACH: Store, motor camp (might close), motel.
HAHEI: Store, motor camp, bkpr hostel/motel. HOT WATER BEACH: The motor camp has closed.
WHENUAKITE: See above.

## 4b. PAEROA - WAIHI - TAURANGA - ROTORUA.    145km

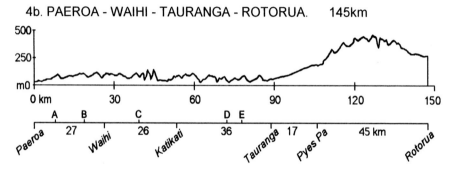

**SERVICES: PAEROA:** See 4a above. **A) KARANGAHAKE:** W end of gorge, tearooms, bkpr hostel.
**B) WAIKINO:** E end of gorge, *i:* Railway Station, pub, picnic area.
**WAIHI:** Alt 50m, pop 3600. *i:* Seddon St ☎ 07 863 6715. Food: All types of outlets.
Accom: Motor camp; motel 2; hotel. Bicycle Shop: Waihi Sports & Cycles, Seddon St ☎ 07 863 8418.
**C) ANTHENREE GORGE:** Tearooms, picnic area.
**KATIKATI:** Alt 30m, pop 2000.Food: All types of outlets. Accom: Motor camp (3½ km S on SH 2 then 3½ km E at Sapphire Springs); bkpr hostel 2; motel.
**D) WHAKAMARAMA:** Store, motor camp (at Omokoroa Beach, 3.5km NE off SH 2).
**E) TE PUNA:** Tearooms, pub.
**TAURANGA:** Alt 5m, pop 45,000. *i:* The Strand ☎ 07 578 8103. Food: All types of outlets.
Accom: Motor camp 3; hostel (bkpr 3, YHA 1); motel many; hotel 4.
Transport: Bus & shuttle to/from just about everywhere south of Auckland.
Bicycle Shop: *Hedgehog Bikes, Cnr Cameron Rd & 4th Ave ☎ 07 578 7554. *Bikes Direct, 633 Cameron Rd ☎ 07 578 2441. *Koop's Cycles, Cnr Seventeenth Ave & Cameron Rd ☎ 07 578 5406.
**MT MAUNGANUI:** Alt 5m, pop 15,000. *i:* Salisbury Ave ☎ 07 575 5099. Food: All types of outlets.
Accom: Motor camp 4; bkpr hostel 2; motel 8; hotel 1. **ROTORUA:** See page 27-28.

**GRADIENTS:** Flat leaving Paeroa then a moderate hill before Mackaytown. A gentle climb through Karangahake Gorge, there is a tunnel & walkway to Waikino along the old railway line if the traffic becomes too much. Bikes are not supposed to be on it but it's much less dangerous if you're challenged! You can always walk your bike on it!

Rolls a little from Waikino to Waihi then alternating stretches of rolls and undulations, some quite long, most of the way to Tauranga. Around Anthenree Gorge the hills are longer and bends more acute. Note: SH 2 between Waihi & Tauranga has a reputation for heavy and sometimes dangerous traffic and called "Suicide Highway" by some! Weekends may be the best time.

The first 17 km on leaving Tauranga is a predominantly gradual climb to Pyes Pa, from there it becomes rolling and undulating, mostly uphill for another 16 km to 500m. The remaining gravel road at the top at Ngawero has now been tar-sealed. A steep 1 km descent into Mangarewa Scenic Reserve and a 1½ km steep to quite steep climb out. Rolls, then another short steep descent and ascent. Rolls and undulates down to Lake Rotorua then mostly gentle terrain to Rotorua.

**ATTRACTIONS:** After Paeroa and their big bottle, pass through Karangahake Gorge, the southern border of the Coromandel Ranges. Plenty of relics from the gold mining period litter this scenic gorge, including the old railway line which is now a walking track and may be safer to walk your bike along this than ride SH 2. See the amazing hole Waihi has dug for itself, with tours by arrangement. On the way to Tauranga are several beach holiday resorts, all a few km off the highway on side roads to the harbour. SH 2 passes through scenic Anthenree Gorge and mural town Katikati which has nearby Saphire hot springs. Rumour has it some dub this stretch of SH 2 as "Suicide Highway"!! It has been suggested week-ends may be best because there are less trucks on the road.

Tauranga is a bustling city and port with nearby Mt Maunganui a popular holiday resort especially with drunken louts at New Year. On the way to the volcanic plateau pass Gate Pa, an historic site from the land wars of last century. Go through several scenic reserves including the spectacular Mangorewa Ecological Area before descending to Lake Rotorua & city.

**OPTIONS:** **ALTERNATIVE i** WAIHI - WAIHI BEACH - SH 2 (N of TAHAWAI). This is about 10 km longer but quieter than using SH 2. Pass through small seaside settlements clustered around the northern entrance to Tauranga Harbour.
WAIHI BEACH: (Including Island View, Bowentown and Anthree) pop 2000. Food: All types of outlets except supermarket. Accom: Motor camp 4 (one includes hot springs); motel 2; hotel.

**ALTERNATIVE ii** TAURANGA - ROTORUA on SH 2/33. Distance 86 km. This is 24 km longer than Tauranga Direct Road but the highest point is 200m lower.

Rolls and undulates with nothing too serious, from Tauranga to Te Puke and Paengaroa. Head inland from there, climbs gently at first, becoming variable uphill. 2 km after entering the pine plantation SH 33 descends for 1 km before resuming up again for 4 km. It then rolls and meanders along for a while before a final 2½ km variable climb to what is the stiff upper lip of the central volcanic plateau at Paretero Pass (300m). A 1 km descent to Okere Falls then mostly easy gradients from there to Rotorua except a small hill at Okawa Bay.
TAURANGA: See above. PAPAMOA: Alt 10m pop 400. Store, motor camp 2, motel.
TE PUKE: Pop 5200. Food: All types of outlets. Accom: Motor camp; motel.
Bicycle Shop: *Attrills Cycles, 124 Jellico St, ☎ 07 573 7019. RANGIURU: Alt 10m, picnic area.
PAENGAROA: Store, motel. See page 46-47 for direct travel to Eastland.
OTARAMARAE: picnic area. OKERE FALLS: Motor camp, picnic area.
MOUREA: Store, tearooms, pub. OWHATA: Motor camp; motel/tearooms.
ROTORUA: See pages 27-28.

# CENTRAL

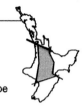

**HIGHLIGHTS** (not in any order of preference):

Rotorua City & surrounding thermal areas

Lake Taupo & Waioreki Thermal Area

Tongariro National Park

Pipiriki & Whanganui River Road

Pureora petrified forest & Pouakani on SH30

Te Aroha & the soda hot spring

Paeroa & Harangahake Gorge

Mangaweka Gorge near Taihape

Waiouru & Desert Road

Rangitaiki & Tapawera on SH5

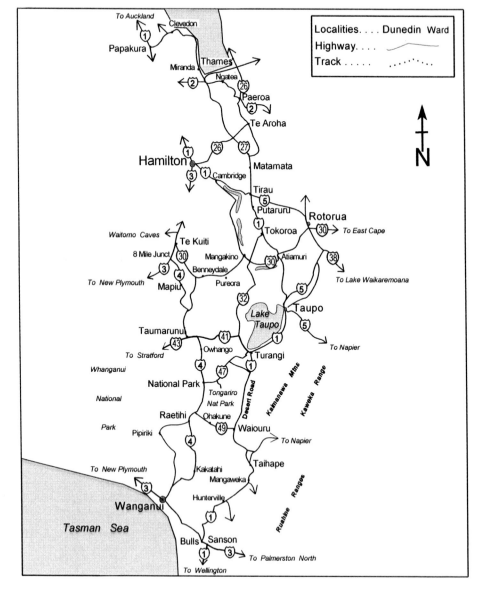

# 5. ROTORUA.

**DIRECTIONS:** There are no suburban trains in Rotorua but the city is small compared to Auckland and Wellington. Mostly gentle to flat gradients within the city.
**SOUTH:** Enter/exit along Fenton St passing Whakarewarewa Thermal Area.
**WEST & NORTH:** Depart the visitor centre and go along Arawa St, right into Ranolf St, left onto Lake Rd and right onto Fairy Springs Rd.
**EAST:** Exit from the visitor centre, go south along Fenton St, left into Amohau St and left again onto Te Ngae Road (SH 30).
**BYPASS** the city centre, going north to south... Continue straight ahead from Fairy Springs Road onto Old Taupo Road, emerging near Whakarewarewa Thermal Area.

**SERVICES: ROTORUA:** Alt 280m, pop 52,000. *i:* Map & Track Shop, 1183 Hinemoa St ☎ 07 349 1845 for track and backpacker info, or 1167 Fenton St ☎ 07 348 5179 for tours.
Food: All types of outlets. Accom: Motor camp 4; bkpr hostel 8; motel heaps; hotel many.
There are also motor camps in the following locations: Ngongaotaha 4; Holden's Bay 2; Hannah's Bay; Blue Lake; Mourea; Okere Falls; Lake Rotoma; Tikitere and Waikite. At Lake Tarawera are 2 DoC camp sites (toilet, water) and Lake Rerewhakaaitu has informal camping.
Transport: Bus & shuttle to/from most places south of Auckland.
Bicycle Shop: *Bike Vegas, 1275 Fenton St ☎ 07 347 1151.
*Rotorua Cycle Centre, 1120 Hinemoa St ☎ 07 348 6588. *Bike Fix, 51 Old Taupo Rd ☎ 07 347 2232.
*Cycle Zone, Cnr Amohau & Hinemaru Sts ☎ 07 348 6610. Not a complete list.

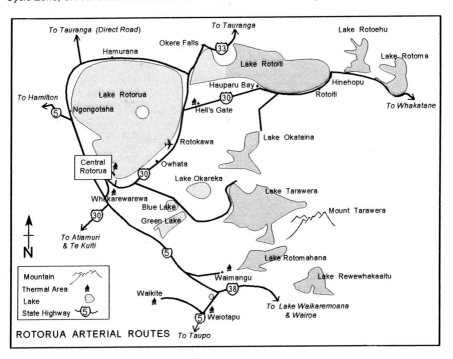

ROTORUA ARTERIAL ROUTES *To Taupo*

**ATTRACTIONS:** Well, without wanting to offend the local promotion body (but probably will), the place stinks! It is a haven for those who ate too many baked beans! Yet in spite of the smell and hype, Rotorua is a fascinating region to visit. Tourists have been coming from all over the world for more than a century to check out the natural wonders, take the waters and observe Maori culture.

Minor thermal activity like bubbling mud, steaming vents, fumaroles and funny smells are a normal everyday occurrence as seen in Government Gardens and are free. Also located here are the Polynesian Pools the imposing Bath House, now an art gallery & museum.

This is one of the best locations for an insight into Maori culture, with a choice of concerts and/or hangi (feast) available. The Arawa Tribe's Ohinemutu Village is an important historic complex, including St Faith's, considered to be one of the best four Maori churches and Tamatatekapua meeting house. At Whakarewarewa (Whaka) is the Maori Institute of Arts and Crafts, a thermal area that includes Pohutu Geyser and a forest park with mountain biking trails.

Apart from Whaka, other thermal areas are: Waimangu & Lake Rotomahana, (near the site of the Pink and White Terraces destroyed in the 1886 Mt Tarawera eruption); Waiotapu and Lady Knox Geyser; and Hell's Gate at Tikitere. These are the better known ones, each with its own character. All have an admission fee and are located east of Rotorua.

Also to the east are many of the region's lakes, each a result of volcanic activitiy. Beyond Lake Rotorua, all adjacent to SH 30 on the way to East Cape and in close proximity to each other are Lakes Rotoiti, Rotoehu and Rotoma. The twin Blue & Green Lakes, with the nearby Lakes Okataina and Okareka, are on the way to Lake Tarawera and Te Wairoa Buried Village. Visits to these may be combined with a trip up Mt Tarawera and to the relatively young Lake Rotomahana. There are many tracks for walking and mountain biking, particularly around Whakarewarewa forest and Lake Tarawera.

Some manufactured attractions include; visits to the Agrodome (not a place for hooligans but where sheep and related activities have become an art form); Fairy, Rainbow and Paradise Valley trout springs; Mt Ngongaotaha and Gondola & Luge, plus a couple of mazes and golf.

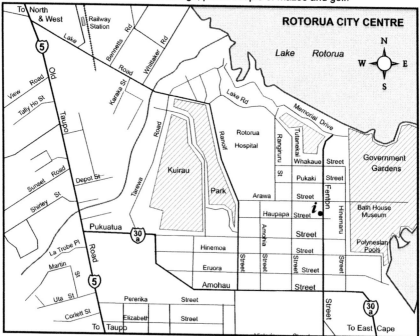

# 6. ROTORUA - TAUPO - NATIONAL PARK - WANGANUI.

| ROUTE: | | SH 1/47/4 | Via River Rd |
|---|---|---|---|
| 6a) ROTORUA - WAIOTAPU - TAUPO | | 80 km | |
| 6b) TAUPO - TURANGI - NATIONAL PARK | | 101 km | |
| 6c) NATIONAL PARK - RAETIHI - WANGANUI | | <u>123 km</u> | 136 km |
| Total | | 304 km | |

**ALTERNATIVE** 6a) i REPOROA - TAUPO on SH 5 or less busy Broadlands Road.

ii ROTORUA - ATIAMURI - TAUPO on SH 30/1, see pages 38-39.

6c) RAETIHI - WANGANUI on SH 4 or more difficult but interesting, partly gravel River Road.

**LINK ROAD** 6b) i TURANGI - WAIOURU on SH 1, see Options page 34.

ii TURANGI - TAUMARUNUI on SH 41. See Options page 36.

## 6a. ROTORUA - TAUPO.    80km

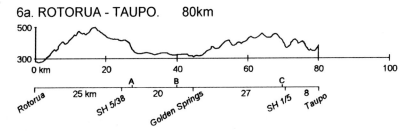

**SERVICES: ROTORUA:** See previous section. **LAKE NGAHEWA:** picnic area.

**A) WAIOTAPU:** Alt 380m, tearooms (at thermal area), hotel. **B) PAREKARANGI:** Alt 310m, store.

**GOLDEN SPRINGS:** Motor camp, store. **WAIKATO RIVER:** Alt 300m, picnic area.

**C) WAIRAKEI:** Alt 370m, dairy, motor camp (no cabins), hotel, picnic area.

**TAUPO:** Alt 360m, pop 18,000. *i:* Tongariro St ☎ 07 378 9000. Food: All types of outlets.

Accom: Motor camp 4; hostel (bkpr 4, YHA 1); motels; hotels.

Transport: Bus & shuttle to/from Auckland, Napier & Wellington. Bicycle Shop: *Corner Shop Cycle & Sports, Horomatangi St ☎ 07 378 7381. *Cycle World, 126 Ruapehu St ☎ 07 378 6117.

**GRADIENTS:** SH 5 rolls and undulates mostly, but not always, uphill out of Rotorua. At SH 5/38 junction, go right (south). A gentle descent becomes quite steep in places for 5 km and passing Waiotapu. After levelling out easy gradients for much of the way to Waikato River. Long sweeping rolls develop as SH 5 meanders through part of the vast Kaingaroa forest, becoming more pronounced around Wairakei, with a final quite steep descent to cross Waikato River and short up into Taupo.

**ATTRACTIONS:** Pass Waimangu, Waiotapu and Wairakei thermal areas on the way to Taupo as well as the Kaingaroa forest plantation. Wairakei area has Craters of the Moon, Huka Falls & Aratiatia Rapids, all close to each other and easily accessible from Taupo. A number of other attractions here are: jet boating, helicopter flights, horse treks, vintage river boat rides, rafting, a prawn farm etc. Farther afield is Orakei Korako Hidden Valley, another thermal area some claim as the best.

Taupo is a pleasant town and a less smelly and commercialised alternative to Rotorua. Other activities around Taupo are bungy jumping, tandem sky-diving, A.C. (Armed Constabulary) Baths, white-water rafting, kayaking, several walks and lake cruises. Taupo is New Zealand's biggest lake, a huge active volcano (See Section 6b) and source of the longest river, the Waikato. It travels over 400 km to reach the Tasman Sea south of Auckland and from which much of the North Island's hydro power comes. Oh yes, mustn't forget the trout fishing - after all, it's said to be the best in the world!

**OPTIONS: ALTERNATIVE i** REPOROA - BROADLANDS - TAUPO. Distance 48 km.
Avoids most of the rolling hills on SH 5, is 2 km longer, has less traffic and scenically there is little difference. Turn off SH 5 onto Settlers Road, which after REPOROA: (Alt 290m, store) becomes Broadlands Road.

## 6b. TAUPO - TURANGI - NATIONAL PARK. 101km

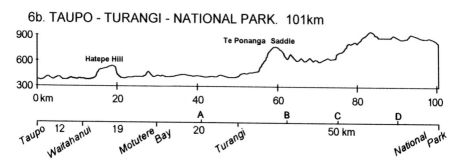

**SERVICES: TAUPO:** See above. **WAITAHANUI:** Alt 360m, dairy, motor camp, motel 2.
**HATEPE:** Dairy. **MOTUTERE BAY:** Store/motor camp (no cabins).
**MISSION BAY:** Picnic area (tables). **TE RANGIITA:** Alt 360m. Dairy, motor camp; motel 2.
**A) MOTUOAPA:** Dairy, tearooms, takeaways, domain motor camp (no cabins); motel.
**TURANGI:** Alt 380m, pop 4000. *i:* Ngawaka Place ☎ 07 386 8999. Food: All types of outlets.
Accom: Motor camp 2; bkpr hostel 2; motel 6; hotel 2. **TE PONANGA SADDLE:** Picnic area.
**B) LAKE ROTOAIRA:** Alt 560m, picnic area.
**C) JUNCT SH 46/47:** Alt 660m,Tearooms/takeaways, cabins (also tent sites).
**D) WHAKAPAPA VILLAGE:** (6 km UP SH 48). *i:* Park HQ ☎ 07 892 3729. Store, motor camp, motel, hotel. **MANGAHUIA:** Alt 880m, DoC camping (toilet, water, table), adj SH 47.
**NATIONAL PARK:** Alt 820m, pop 300. Food: Store, dairy. Accom: Bkpr hostel 5; motels 3; hotel.
Transport: Train stops operating at the end of September. Bus & shuttle to/from Auck & Wgtn.

**GRADIENTS:** Mostly undulates alongside Lake Taupo to Turangi, apart from a variable steep 150m climb and steep descent at Hatepe Hill (510m), with another smaller hill at Ohoumahanga Pt. The entire route is blessed with picnic areas at regular intervals.
Flat for the first 4 km on leaving Turangi then a steep climb of 360m in 6 km to Te Ponanga Saddle (740m), followed by a shorter but equally steep descent to Lake Rotoaira. After several more rolls of ever decreasing gradients to Raewaehu Canal, SH 47 settles down to gentle terrain until the junction with Rangipo Rd, (SH 47a). Note: The steep hill over Te Ponanga Saddle can be avoided by taking SH 1 from Turangi and going right onto the mostly rolling Rangipo Road.
A mostly (but not all) variable climb goes through the high country to the meridian point of SH 47 at Mangatepopo Road (910m), then mostly gentle rolls and undulations passing Whakapapa turn off, before going left onto SH 4 at National Park Village.

**ATTRACTIONS:** Taupo is the heart shaped lake in the heart of the North Island and although seemingly tranquil, sometimes beats with passion. Does that sound corny? Well how about this then? Ponder as you pedal past pretty picture postcard pviews that you're actually on the lip of a huge active volcano. In about 185AD an eruption occurred that completely devastated the surrounding area in a 80 km radius. The force of the blast was so great it reached speeds of more than 700 kph and temperatures over 800°c. The effects are still visible today. Scientists now estimate 150 km³ of material was ejected and in some places lies over 100m deep. This is 150 times bigger than the Mt St Helens eruption a decade ago. They have also found there has been two earlier eruptions in the last ¼ million years that were between 2 and 10 times bigger than the last. Phew!

Anyway, today small settlements dot the lake shore waiting to be obliterated by the next monster. In the meantime they mostly cater for visiting holiday makers and fishermen. Turangi and Tokaanu have noted hot springs and a trout hatchery.

The panoramic view over Lake Taupo from Te Ponanga Saddle is worth the effort, perhaps. Tongariro comprises of several volcanic mountains and was the first of New Zealand's many national parks, formed in 1887 after being gifted to the nation by Ngati Tuwharetoa Tribe. Popular activities are skiing in winter and tramping in summer. Apart from distant Turangi, main bases for activities are Whakapapa, National Park and Ohakune. They are located on the west and south of the mountains and provide a wide range of services for park users. Grand Château at Whakapapa is a hotel with a refined air quite uncommon in New Zealand, the nearby golf course is the highest in the country. Beware bees between Turangi and National Park.

Apart from the short walks around Whakapapa village, the most frequented track is the Tongariro Crossing. It goes between Mangatepopo Road and Ketetahi Springs and is alleged to be "the finest one day walk in New Zealand". The multi-day Northern Circuit (a DoC Great Walk) and the Round the Mountain Track are for the more adventurous. As for any mountain environment, care needs to be taken regarding weather conditions and to use appropriate equipment. Here also requires an eye open for other unusual activity. Mt Ruapehu became quite active during late 1995 but it has since calmed down. The trail up to crater lake may be closed if eruptions recommence.

## 6c. NATIONAL PARK - RAETIHI - WANGANUI. 123km

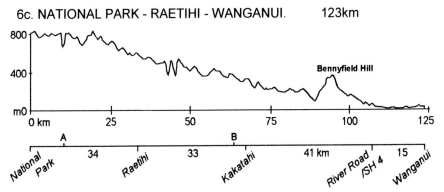

**SERVICES: NATIONAL PARK:** See previous section. **A) MAKATOTE VIADUCT:** Picnic areas.
**RAETIHI:** Alt 520m, pop 1400. Food: All types of outlets except supermarket.
Accom: Motor camp; motel/hotel.
**B) RAUKAWA FALLS:** picnic area. Accom at YMCA camp 1km south of the falls, 4km north of....
**KAKATAHI:** Alt 200m, store/tearooms, bkpr hostel (3 km S). **RIVER ROAD JUNCT:** picnic area.
**WANGANUI:** See pages 61 to 65 for onward travel.

**GRADIENTS:** SH 4 rolls and undulates, more down than up from National Park to Carrot Corner, apart from a steep 80m descent in 1½ km and 60m ascent in 1 km to cross Makatote Stream at the viaduct. Mostly down after Carrot Corner to and beyond Raetihi before a steep 1km descent to cross Mangawhero River. Climbs for 2 km, with a steep 2 km descent to cross Ararawa River, followed by a 1 km climb. 10 km before Kakatahi is a variable 4 km descent, becomes rolling downhill and easing to gentle gradients. On leaving Mangawhero Valley, a sometimes steep and winding climb over Bennyfield Hill (280m) is required, followed by a similar descent before gradually easing. Mostly flat for the last part into Wanganui, travelling alongside Whanganui River.

**ATTRACTIONS:** Raetihi is at one end of the Whanganui River Road and near to Tongariro National Park. Between Raetihi and Wanganui on SH 4 is Mangawhero Valley. Apart from a few views and the beautiful Raukawa Falls, near the one and only tiny settlement of Kakatahi, there is little in the way of attractions or vehicles. Try the partly gravel Whanganui River Road, see alternative below.

Wanganui is a city of 40,000 straddling Whanganui River and a gateway to Whanganui National Park. Durie Hill Tower has splendid views over the city and on clear days Mt Ruapehu can be seen. Putiki Church is regarded as one of the finest Maori churches. A group held a land protest in Moutua Gardens during 1995, and somebody stole a statue!

**OPTIONS: LINK ROAD** WANGANUI - BULLS.   Distance: 43 km. See Page 61 for details.

## 6c ALTERNATIVE: RAETIHI - PIPIRIKI - WANGANUI.   136km

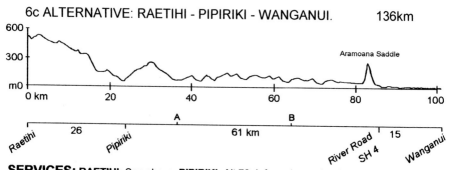

**SERVICES: RAETIHI:** See above. **PIPIRIKI:** Alt 70, Informal camping (shelter, toilet, water). **RIVER VIEW:** Alt 200m, picnic area, informal camping. **A) HIRUHARAMA:** (Jerusalem) Alt 50m. **RANANA:** Kauika campground (showers, toilets, kitchen, no cabins), check it is open at Raetihi or Wanganui. **B) OTUMAIRE:** DoC camping (toilet, water). **ARAMOANA SADDLE:** Alt 230m, picnic area. **SH 4/RIVER ROAD JUNCT:** Alt 20m, picnic area. **WANGANUI:** See page 60-62 for onward travel.

**GRADIENTS:** Generally rolls downhill from Raetihi except for a moderate climb, before a fairly long and sometimes steep descent to Pipiriki. After Pipiriki climb to River View then rolls and undulates alongside the river. To leave the valley climb 200m in 2½ km on another highway to heaven, to go over Aramoana Saddle. Descends by a similar amount to join SH 4, then almost flat to Wanganui.

**ATTRACTIONS:** After Pipiriki travel alongside the often spectacular Whanganui River for many km on a normally quiet but gravel highway with about half unsealed. It is 13 km longer than SH 4 and much longer in time. Last century before the development of roads and rail, Whanganui River was an important link to the interior of the North Island and had considerable traffic on it.

Many of the localities were named after famous overseas places, such as: Atene (Athens), Ranana (London), Koriniti (Corinth) and Hiruharama (Jerusalem). Jerusalem has an historic 100 year old convent. Interpretation displays are at points of interest along the valley and an informative leaflet is also available. A couple of walkways line the route. The River Road travels along only the lower reaches of Whanganui River National Park. The bulk and more spectacular parts are upstream inaccessible by road. It is possible to canoe down river from Taumarunui to Pipiriki or Wanganui.

# 7. BULLS - NATIONAL PARK - TE KUITI - ROTORUA.

| ROUTE: | SH 1/49/4/30 | SH 1 |
|---|---|---|
| 7a) BULLS - WAIOURU - NATIONAL PARK | 175 km | |
| 7b) NATIONAL PARK - TAUMARUNUI - TE KUITI | 125 km | |
| 7c) TE KUITI - ATIAMURI - ROTORUA | 146 km | |
| link TAUPO - ATIAMURI - TIRAU - HAMILTON | _____ | 153 km |
| Total | 446 km | |

**LINK ROAD** 7a) i PALMERSTON NORTH - MANGAWEKA. See South, Section 15b, Options (Page 62). Also use this as an alternative to SH 1 for part of the way to Wellington.

ii WAIOURU - TURANGI on SH 1 (Desert Rd, Page 34-35).

iii TAIHAPE - NAPIER on the partly gravel Old Napier - Taihape Road, (Page 55).

7b) TAUMARUNUI - TURANGI on SH 41 (Page 36).

7c) i WHAKAMARU - TURANGI on SH 32. West of Lake Taupo (Page 37).

ii MANGAKINO - CAMBRIDGE on various (sealed) back roads. This can also be part of an alternative to SH 1 between Taupo and Hamilton (Page 37).

## 7a. BULLS - WAIOURU - NATIONAL PARK. 175km

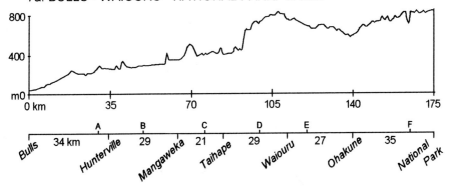

**SERVICES: BULLS:** See page 60-61. **MARTON:** 3 km W of SH 1, pop 5000.
Food: All types of outlets. Accom: Motor camp; motel 2; hotel. **A) BRUCE PARK:** picnic area.
**HUNTERVILLE:** Alt 280m, pop 600. Dairy, tearooms, motel, hotel.
**VINEGAR HILL:** Alt 310m, domain camping (toilets, water) down by river.
**MAKOHINE VIADUCT:** Alt 280m, picnic area. **B) OHINGAITI:** Alt 280m, hotel.
**FLAT HILLS:** Tearooms. **MANGAWEKA HILL:** picnic area.
**MANGAWEKA:** Alt 350m, pop 500. *i:* DoC ☎ 06 382 5824. Tearooms, domain camp (down by river); motel; hotel. **MANUI:** Alt 500m, picnic area. **C) UTIKU:** Alt 375m, the hotel has closed.

**TAIHAPE:** Alt 440m, pop 2200. *i:* 90 Hautapu St ☎ (06) 388 0350.
Food: All types of outlets. Accom: Motor camp (3 km N); bkpr hostel; motel 3; hotel.
**D) HIHITAHI:** picnic area. **IRIRINGI:** picnic area (tables).
**WAIOURU:** Alt 810m, pop 3000. Food: All types of outlets except supermarket.
Accom: Motel, hotel/motel. **E) TANGIWAI:** picnic area.
**OHAKUNE:** Alt 590m, pop 1500. *i:* 54 Clyde St ☎ 06 385 8427. Food: All types of outlets except
supermarket. Accom: Motor camp; hostel (bkpr 1, YHA 1); motel 6; hotel 3.
**F) MAKATOTE VIADUCT:** picnic areas.
**NATIONAL PARK:** Alt 820m, pop 300. Food: All types of outlets except supermarket.
Accom: Bkpr hostel 5; motels 3; hotel. Transport: Train stop operating at the end of September. Bus
& shuttle to/from Auckland & Wellington.

**GRADIENTS:** Almost flat uphill for much of the way from Bulls to Hunterville, except for an odd
descent, such as at Porewa, with hills slowly closing in. Between Hunterville and Taihape are several
hills to cross as the highway passes through papa country of steep river cliffs. Vinegar, Mangaweka and
Manui Hills are the more notable hills, some having, long, steep gradients of several km, both up and
down. These are separated by rolling and undulating country as SH 1 passes through Ohingaiti,
Mangaweka and Utiku.

The first 5 km out of Taihape are generally rolling, more up than down, then starts a long variable
steep 6 km climb to Turangarere, only broken by a short stretch of downhill part way. After gradients
ease, ascend gently alongside Hautapu River, before entering rolling country as SH 1 passes through
low hills and ending flat to undulating into Waiouru.

After leaving SH 1 at Waiouru, SH 49 becomes a stepped downhill until Tangiwai Stream, then
predominantly rolling country before giving way to a gradual undulating descent into Ohakune. Flat
leaving Ohakune, then a mostly variable ascent to Carrot Corner, go right off SH 49. SH 4 rolls and
undulates, more up than down for most of the way to National Park, apart from a steep 60m descent
in 1 km and 80m ascent in 1½ km to cross Makatote Stream at the viaduct.

**ATTRACTIONS:** Flat ~~boring~~ fertile farming country around Bulls. After Hunterville enter classique
papa (mudstone) country of Rangitaikei River. Mangaweka is an historic village with low flying tearooms
and surrounded by spectacular, steep and deep river cliffs. Gumboot Taihape claims to be the
quintessential rural town. Waiouru is an army base surrounded by high country tussockland in an often
bleak and windswept setting and a brooding volcano nearby.

There is a military museum with a memorial that is the world's biggest greenstone structure - and
subject to investigations regarding illegal mining. At Tangiwai there is a memorial to New Zealand's
worst rail disaster where 151 people died on Christmas Eve 1953. Pass through carrot country, as is
evident at Ohakune. Ohakune and National Park are two of the villages catering to the needs of users
of Tongariro National Park. See page 30-31.

**OPTIONS: LINK ROAD i** WAIOURU - SUMMIT 21 km. SUMMIT - TURANGI. Distance: 42 km.
WAIOURU: See above. SUMMIT: picnic area. OTURERE STREAM: picnic area.
MANGATAWAI STREAM: picnic area. TURANGI: See page 30-31.

Gentle gradients on leaving Waiouru, then a short descent followed by a moderate quite steep climb,
easing to towards the top to reach the highest stretch of sealed highway in New Zealand at 1075m.
After the summit SH 1 becomes a short, steep roller coaster descent to Outerere Stream, then the
Desert Road descent begins in earnest. It drops in a series of steps, often steep and long with hair-pin
bends and substantial climbs to cross several streams. 14 km from Turangi, shortly before Puketara
Stream, starts a long gradual mostly easy descent to Turangi.

SH 1 between Turangi and Waiouru is called the Desert Road as it runs east of Tongariro National Park. It is called that to confuse people, because although things are pretty bleak, it isn't really a desert. Wild horses and military men are sometimes seen around these parts, but who put those power lines there? The main access points to Tongariro National Park are from west and south of the mountain. Interesting layering in the road cuttings from volcanic activity.

## 7b. NATIONAL PARK - TAUMARUNUI - TE KUITI  125km

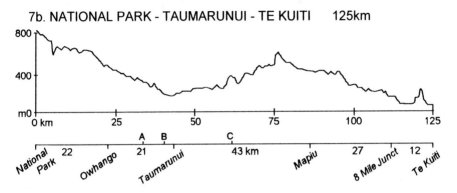

**SERVICES: NATIONAL PARK:** See previous section.

**OWHANGO:** Alt 440m, pop 250. Tearooms, dairy, bkpr hostel.

**A) PIRIAKA:** Store. **B) MANUNUI:** Alt 180m, motel/restaurant.

**TAUMARUNUI:** Alt 170m, pop 6500. *i:* Railway Station ☎ 07 895 7494. Food: All types of outlets. Accom: Motor camp (4 km S); motel 3; hotel 3 (one has bkpr accom). Bicycle Shop: Paramount Cycles, Hakiaha St ☎ 07 895 8846.

**C) OKAHUKURA:** Alt 200m, picnic area. **MAPIU:** Store/tearooms.

**TE KUITI:** Alt 60m, pop 4900. *i:* Rora St ☎ 07 878 8077. Food: All types of outlets. Accom: Motor camp; domain camping 2 (toilets, water, donation payment); bkpr hostel; motel; hotel. Transport: Train to/from Auckland & Wellington stop operating at the end of September. Bus & shuttle to/from New Plymouth, Auck & Wgtn.

**WAITOMO CAVES:** 20 km north west. See page 69-70.


**GRADIENTS:** On leaving National Park SH 4 starts with gentle gradients but soon becomes rolling with a 2 km long steep and winding drop at Raurimu and a variable up again before levelling out to undulate and roll. After Oio (yes Oio) Overbridge is a 10 km gradual descent passing through Owhango (yes Owhango) on the way. Long sweeping rolls take over before Piriaka, ending with a quite steep 2 km drop. The last 10 km to Taumarunui is mostly gentle down to flat.

A gentle ascent on leaving Taumarunui for several km then becomes rolling around Okahukura, with one particular stiff winding 5 km climb, the middle part being through a narrow gorge. A short 1 km steep descent to cross Ahura River, then undulations before a final 2½ km, some steep climb, to Hiwi Saddle (600m). Starts steep down then becomes a steady gradual descent to Mapiu. After Mapiu becomes rolling with 1 km climb to Kopaki turn off and a variable steep 4 km descent. Apart from a 3 km rolling stretch, the last 12 km of SH 4 to 8 Mile Junction is mostly flat. Go right onto SH 3, with a flattish 12 km into Te Kuiti, apart from a moderate descent, two steep steps up and a final sheepish swoop down into town - not all that flat really.

**ATTRACTIONS:** Splendid views, in fine weather, of Tongariro National Park, the first of New Zealand's many national parks. See page 30. Enjoy the plunge past the Raurimu Spiral, a wonder of not so modern engineering. Taumarunui is the main departure point for travelling on Whanganui River National Park. Go by kayak or canoe, jetboat or inflatable doll, independent or guided, several hours or multi-day. There are plenty of narrow gorges, waterfalls, side streams, caves, native bush and historical sites to explore. See abundant birdlife, possums, super-sonic bats and possibly an underwater goat with snorkels and flippers.

Expect to take up to a week to do the 145 km to Pipiriki, which has most of the spectacular scenery. There are other in-out options and an information leaflet is available that describes some of them. The main tramping tracks are Matemateaonga and Mangapurua, they run generally east to west and both have one end in the river. The latter has the Bridge to Nowhere, a 40 minute walk from the river end. As with some of the other DoC Great Walks, the rules and fee structure must have been dreamed up by clueless marketing men and bureaucrats. Who else would call a journey by river a "Great Walk" and make compliance so complicated? Seek up to date information and pay before departure, or else!

Between Taumarunui and Te Kuiti is classic King Country and not much else. Te Kuiti is another rural town and thinks it's the shearing capital of the world. The statue is of a sheep and does not resemble Jim the local ex-Prime Minister in any way. Te Kooti, a noted rebel of the land wars period lived here for many years and gave the local tribe their beautiful Te Tokanganui a Noho Marae.

For information on Waitomo Caves and north, see page 70.

**OPTIONS: LINK ROAD i** TAUMARUNUI - TURANGI on SH 41. Distance: 66 km.

Easy gradients to Pungapunga then climbs most of the 15 km, becoming steep in places, to Waituhi Saddle (870m). The lookout affords spectacular views of Tongariro, King Country and Mt Egmont. Heads downhill in variable steps after the saddle for most of the 14 km to Kuratau Junct (470m). Then two long quite steep rolls before resuming a steep down, this time to negotiate Waihi Bluff. Then mostly gentle undulations from the bottom of the bluff to Turangi. There are thermal pools at Tokaanu.
TAUMARUNUI: See Section 3b for details. WAITUHI SADDLE: Alt 870m, picnic area.
TOKAANU: Takeaways, dairy, motor camp, motel, hotel. TURANGI: See page 29.
For Taumarunui - Stratford on SH 43, see page 65-66.

## 7c.  TE KUITI - ATIAMURI - ROTORUA.    146km

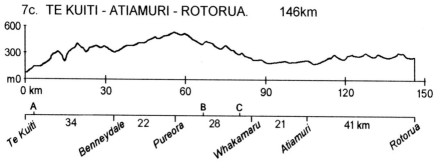

**SERVICES: TE KUITI:** See above. **A) MANGAOKEWA:** Domain camping (water, toilet).
**BENNEYDALE:** Alt 310m, store, takeaways, pub.
**PUREORA:** Alt 560m. DoC camping (toilets, water, table, shelter). **B) POUAKANI:** picnic area.
**C) MANGAKINO:** 3 km off SH 30, alt 220m, pop 700. Store, tearooms, domain camping (toilet) hotel.
**WHAKAMARU:** Alt 240m, Store, tearooms. **ATIAMURI:** Alt 260m, tearooms, bkpr hostel, picnic area (toilets, water, shelter). **ROTORUA:** See page 27-28.

**GRADIENTS:** Gentle gradients around Mokau River, between Mangapehi and Benneydale, and at Pureora, otherwise rolls and undulates, sometimes long and quite steep, more up than down. After Pureora SH 30 rolls and undulates, more down than up to Whakamaru, then easy gradients to Atiamuri. At Atiamuri go left on SH 1, then right onto SH 30 to Rotorua. Continues with more of the same terrain going for much of the way to Rotorua.

**ATTRACTIONS:** A few km out of Te Kuiti is a local beauty spot of Mangaokewa Scenic Reserve. Pass through limestone country on the way to Pureora. Pureora State Forest has several tramps and a fascinating buried forest. The blast from the Taupo eruption of 185 AD flattened the existing forest in seconds, covering it under a thick layer of ash and pumice. So instant and complete was the effect that the fallen trees and even vegetation were preserved. The remains of this ancient forest can be seen a few km off SH 30 near forest HQ. Farther east in the Kinleith forest plantation and down a short track is 'Pouakani', the largest known living totara tree and dates from the Taupo eruption. There is some dramatic scenery around Atiamuri.

**OPTIONS: LINK ROAD i** WHAKAMARU - TURANGI on SH 32. Distance: 90 km.
On the west side of Lake Taupo. It can also be an extension of Link Road ii below. Very hilly in places with some long steep stretches, particularly after Tihoi. At Kuratau Junction go left, with two long rolling hills before descending the steep Waihi Bluff, then gentle undulations from the bottom to Turangi.
WHAKAMARU: See above. KAKAHO: DoC camping (water, toilet) 3 km off SH 32. TIHOI: Store.
TOKAANU: Takeaways, dairy, motor camp, 3 motel, hotel, thermal pools. TURANGI: See Section 16b.

**LINK ROAD ii** MANGAKINO - CAMBRIDGE. Distance: 78 km. 106 km if using it as an alternative to SH 1 between Atiamuri and Cambridge. 16 km longer than SH 1 plus any detours. It can also be an extension of Link Road i above.
Runs south and west of Waikato River and the hydro lakes of Maraetai, Waipapa, Arapuni and Karapiro. A less busy alternative to SH 1. Mostly rolling country. A few quite steep and longish parts between Maratai and Waipapa, from Waipapa up through Mangawhio Gorge, around Wai-iti Stream and Horahora. Actually quite a lot!
MANGAKINO: See above. LAKE WAIPAPA: picnic area (toilet, water, table).
LAKE ARAPUNI: informal camping (toilet, water, table) on west side of lake at Bulmer or Arapuni landings, 2 - 3 km off highway. ARAPUNI: 4 km off highway, across Waikato River, dairy.
LAKE KARAPIRO: Domain motor camp (no cabins), tearooms across Waikato River.
CAMBRIDGE See above.

## 7c LINK iii. ROTORUA - TIRAU - PAEROA.   136km

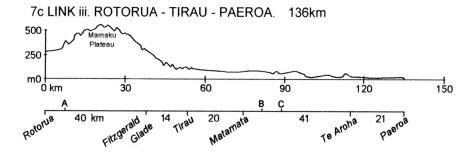

**SERVICES: ROTORUA:** See page 27-28.

**A) NGONGOTAHA:** Store, tearooms, takeaways, dairy, motor camp, hotel.

**FITZGERALD GLADE:** Tearooms/dairy.

**TIRAU:** Alt 115m, pop 500. *i:* Main Road, ☎ 07 883 1202.
Food: All types of outlets except supermarket. Accom: Hotel.

**MATAMATA:** Alt 60m, pop 5800. *i:* 45 Broadway ☎ 07 888 7260. Food: All types of outlets.
Accom:Motel 3; hotel 2. Bicycle Shop: *Extreme Cycle Centre, 63 Arawa St ☎ 07 888 8917.

**B) OKAUIA:** Motor camp incl hot pools, motel. **C) WAIRERE FALLS:** picnic area.

**TE AROHA:** Alt 30m, pop 3500. *i:* 102 Whitaker St ☎ 07 884 8052.
Food: All types of outlets. Accom: Motor camp; YHA hostel; motel; hotel.

**PAEROA:** Alt 15m, pop 3800. *i:* Belmont Rd ☎ 07 862 8636. Food: All types of outlets.
Accom: Motor camp; motel 3; hotel. Transport: Bus & shuttle to/from Auckland, Tauranga & Coromandel
Peninsula. Bicycle Shop: Paeroa Marine & Cycles, 29 Puke Rd ☎ 07 862 7061.

**GRADIENTS:** SH 5 is mostly flat within Rotorua then after Ngongotaha turn off, a rolling climb begins, soon becoming a long, gradual, stepped ascent of the Mamaku Plateau. Rolls and undulates up around 500m for some distance before eventually making its way down past Fitzgerald Glade to Tapapa at the bottom. Rolls and undulates for the last 9 km to Tirau. Mostly flat to Matamata and gentle rolling from there to Te Aroha and continues similar through to Paeroa.

**ATTRACTIONS:** After Rotorua cross the Mamaku Plateau, passing the pleasant Fitzgerald Glade on the way down the far side and enter the rich fertile farming country of the Waikato. Tirau is a cross roads town, nearby are the Okoroire hot springs. After Tirau is Matamata another cow town, with historic Firth Tower and Hobbiton located nearby. On the way to Te Aroha are Okauia & Opal Hot Springs, beyond there a short way off Old Te Aroha Rd, Wairere Falls entertain with 150m drop.

   At one time Te Aroha was a serious rival to Rotorua as New Zealand's première thermal resort but got left behind and with it a charm lacking in many other towns. In the Domain are thermal pools and the world's only hot soda geyser. Mt Te Aroha (Mountain of Love) is the highest point on the Kaimai-Mamaku Range and has spectacular views across the Hauraki Plains. On clear days distant mountains of Moehau, Egmont & Tongariro are visible. Paeroa once a port town before the swamp was drained, is famous for Lemon and Paeroa (L&P), New Zealand's very own soft drink, although Paeroa mineral water is no longer used. See the bottle at the end of town. The spectacular Karangahake Gorge and walkway is on the way to Waihi.

**OPTIONS: ALTERNATIVE i** TAPAPA - MATAMATA via OKOROIRE: hotel/motor camp (no cabins), hot springs. This route avoids Tirau and can be used to miss out Matamata as well.

**ALTERNATIVE ii** MATAMATA - MIRANDA on SH 27. Distance: 86 km
Save 17 km on this direct but busier, less interesting route to Auckland, missing out Te Aroha and Paeroa. It has a few steep rolling hills between Pateonga and Mangatarata (SH 2) otherwise mostly flat. Go left on SH 2 for 3 km, then right onto SH 25. This goes to Waitakaruru, go left to Miranda.
WAHAROA: Store, takeaways, tearooms, motor camp. TATUANUI: Dairy/takeaways.
MORRINSVILLE: 8 km off SH 27. Alt 15m, pop 5500. *i:* Thames St ☎ 07 889 5575.
Food: All types of outlets. Accom: Domain motor camp (no cabins); motel; hotel.
Bicycle Shop: Kaimai Cycles, 237 Thames St ☎ 07 889 6210.

# 7c LINK iv: TAUPO - ATIAMURI - TIRAU - HAMILTON.  153km

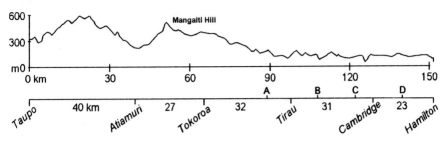

**SERVICES: TAUPO:** See page 29.
**ATIAMURI:** Alt 260m, tearooms, bkpr hostel, picnic area (toilet, water, table, shelter).
**TOKOROA:** Alt 380m, pop 18,000. *i:* SH 1 ☎ 07 886 8872. Food: All types of outlets.
Accom: Motor camp; motel 4; hotel. Bicycle Shop: Sth Waikato Cycles, Rosebery St ☎ 07 886 9178.
**A) PUTARURU:** Alt 160m, pop 4300. Food: All types of outlets except supermarket.
Accom: Motor camp; bkpr hostel; motel; hotel.
**TIRAU:** Alt 115m, pop 600. *i:* Main Road, ☎ 07 883 1202.
Food: All types of outlets except supermarket. Accom: Hotel.
**B) PIARERE:** Tearooms. **C) LAKE KARAPIRO:** Tearooms, domain motor camp (no cabins) over river.
**CAMBRIDGE:** Alt 40m, pop 8500. Food: All types of outlets. Accom: Domain motor camp; bkpr hostel;
motel 4; hotel 3. Bicycle Shop: Four Seasons Mowers & Cycles, 57 Duke St ☎ 07 827 6763.
**D) TAMAHERE:** Alt 30m. Store, pub, motel. **HAMILTON:** See page 69.

**GRADIENTS:** After a short dip leaving Taupo, SH 1 climbs quite steep for 1 km, then rolls to the SH
5/1 junction. Go left onto SH 1, and starts a long variable and rolling uphill. Then alternates between
rolling and undulating, sometimes quite long and quite steep, more down than up, but nothing extra
special. Continues in this non-descript way until after Atiamuri when SH 1 climbs 5 km to cross
Maungaiti Hill (530m), then goes down variably for 1½ km before return to the previous terrain. This
time it rolls and undulates down most of the way to Tirau. Tirau is a cross roads town, to Auckland
(north) and Rotorua (east) see Section 18a. Undulates and rolls all the way from Tirau to Hamilton.

**ATTRACTIONS:** Several km off SH 1 between Taupo and Atiamuri is Orakei Korako and the
Hidden Valley, a thermal area some consider one of the best in New Zealand. Around Atiamuri is the
Kinleith plantation forest, Ohakuri hydro power scheme and Pohaturoa Recreational Reserve, with
some dramatic scenery thrown in. Next is Kinleith Mill, 8km south of timber town Tokoroa, that
processes logs from the surrounding forests. Putaruru has a timber museum and Tirau is a cross roads
town. Lake Karapiro is another of the many man-made lakes built to feed several power stations found
along Waikato River. It's also the North Island's main rowing centre with regattas held regularly.
Cambridge is a horse breeding centre and Hamilton a cow cocky town. See page 69.

# EAST

**HIGHLIGHTS** (not in any order of preference):

Te Urewera National Park
Northern East Cape coastline
Te Puia Springs & Tokomaru Bay
Tolaga Bay & Cook's Cove
Waioeka Gorge

Gisborne and local beaches
Views of White Island from Bay of Plenty
Morere Springs & Mahia Peninsula
St Mary's Church, Tikitiki
Lake Tutira, Mohaka River & Viaduct on SH2

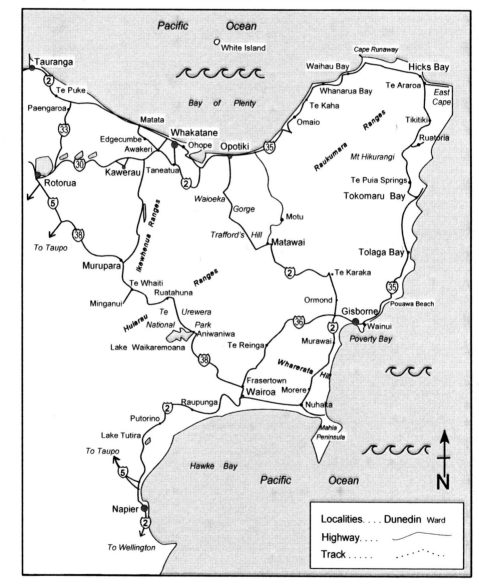

Localities. . . . Dunedin Ward
Highway. . . . .
Track . . . . .

# 8. ROTORUA - OPOTIKI - EAST CAPE - GISBORNE.

**ROUTE:** SH 30/35

| | |
|---|---|
| 8a) ROTORUA - OPOTIKI | 130 km |
| 8b) OPOTIKI - HICKS BAY | 148 km |
| 8b) HICKS BAY - GISBORNE | 182 km |
| Total | 460 km |

**ALTERNATIVE** 8a) AWAKERI - KUTARERE on SH 2 through Whakatane.
**SIDE TRIP** 8b) TE ARAROA - EAST CAPE.
**LINK ROAD** 8a) TE TEKO (SH 30) - MURUPARA (SH 38) on Galatea Road.

## 8a. ROTORUA - WHAKATANE - OPOTIKI. 130km

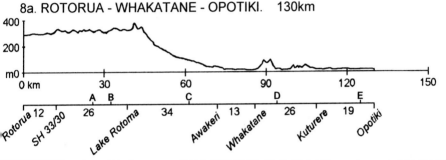

**SERVICES: ROTORUA:** See pages 27-28. **TIKITERE:** (Hell's Gate) The motor camp has closed.
**A) LAKE ROTOITI:** Alt 280m, picnic area at Hauparu Bay. Store, takeaways at Gisborne Pt.
Pub & camping at Hinehopu. **B) LAKE ROTOEHU:** Alt 295m, picnic area.
**LAKE ROTOMA:** Alt 315m, Motor camp; dairy/tearooms/pub/camping, picnic area.
**KAWERAU:** 7 km off SH 30. Alt 30m, pop 8000. *i:* Plunket St, ☎ 07 323 7550.
Food: All types of outlets. Accom: Motel; hotel 2.
Bicycle Shop: Spokes Cycles Centre, Onslow St ☎ 07 323 8418.
**C) TE TEKO:** Alt 25m, store, pub. **AWAKERI:** (junct) Dairy, tearooms. Motor camp with hot springs.
**WHAKATANE:** Alt 5m, pop 13,000. *i:* Boon St ☎ 07 308 6058.
Food: All types of outlets. Accom: Motor camp; bkpr hostel 2; motel 5; hotel 5.
Bicycle Shop: *Whakatane Cycle Centre, Boon St ☎ 07 308 8663.
*Spokes Cycle Centre, 109 The Strand ☎ 07 308 8501.
**D) OHOPE:** Alt 5m, pop 2000. Food: All types of outlets except supermarket.
Accom: Motor camp 2; motel 6; hotel.
**E) WAIOTAHI BEACH:** Alt 5m. Picnic area, store, tearooms, motor camp; bkpr hostel.
**OPOTIKI:** See Section 8b for East Cape (next page), Section 9a for Gisborne direct (page 45).

**GRADIENTS:** Steep hills around Hell's Gate, rolls and undulates past Lakes Rotoiti, Rotoehu and
Rotoma, short steep climb to 370m then descends through native forest to leave the volcanic plateau.
Quite steep and winding at first becomes a gradual descent, flatter as SH 30 passes Kawarau. Flat with
hills falling away and becoming coastal plains nearer to Whakatane. A 120m steep hill separates
Whakatane and Ohope then mostly easy terrain thereafter.

**ATTRACTIONS:** On the way to Whakatane travel past Lakes Rotoiti, Rotoehu and Rotoma, all craters of extinct volcanoes and an indication of the area's violent past. Some thermal activity still remains, such as Hell's Gate. The lakes and bush make this a scenic route to take. After Kawarau with its giant pulp and paper mill, join the plains. Nearby is the distinctive volcanic cone of Mt Edgecumbe. Awakeri is a pleasant spot with the added attraction of hot springs, a short distance from Whakatane.

**OPTIONS: ALTERNATIVE** AWAKERI - KUTARERE on SH 2. Distance 36 km.
Bypasses Whakatane & Ohope Beach but about the same distance. Goes through TANEATUA (Store) and Whakatere Gorge (picnic area), mostly rolling to KUTARERE.

**LINK ROAD** TE TEKO (SH 30) - MURUPARA (SH 38) on Galatea Road. Distance 64 km.
Gives access to/from Whakatane and Te Urewera National Park. Climbs in leaps and bounds through pine plantations, native bush, past hydro lakes and swift flowing rivers. Almost deserted but sealed road. LAKE ANIWHENUA: Alt 150m, picnic area (toilet, water, table). KOPURIKI: Store, tearooms. MURUPARA: See page 47.

## 8b. OPOTIKI - TE KAHA - HICKS BAY.    148km

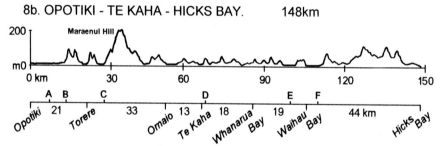

**SERVICES: OPOTIKI:** Alt 5m, pop 6000. *i:* Cnr St John/Elliot Sts ☎ 07 315 8484.
Food: All types of outlets. Accom: Motor camp; bkpr hostel; motel 2; hotel 2.
Bicycle Shop: Marine & Cycle Centre, 90 Church St ☎ 07 315 5758.
**A) TIROHANGA:** Alt 10m, dairy, motor camp.
**B) OPAPE:** Alt 10m, motor camp (no cabins). **TORERE:** Alt 5m, takeaways, picnic area.
**C) HAWAI BAY:** Motor camp/small store. **MARAENUI HILL:** Alt 218m. picnic area.
**OMAIO:** Alt 10m, pop 200. Store/tearooms? Domain camping (toilets, water, table).
**TE KAHA:** Alt 20m, pop 300. Store, motor camp, hotel. **D) MARAETAI BAY:** picnic area.
**WHANARUA BAY:** motor camp/shop, bkpr hostel, takeaways. **E) RAUKOKORE:** picnic area.
**WAIHAU BAY:** Store/tearooms/takeaways, hotel (also cabins). **F) ORUAITI BEACH:** Motor camp.
**HICKS BAY:** Store, takeaways, bkpr hostel, motel. Shuttle to/from Opotiki & Gisborne.

**GRADIENTS:** The first 12 km out of Opotiki are flat. Then 16 km of roller coaster road before a sometimes steep climb from Hawai River to Maraenui Lookout and another to Maraenui Hill (218m), followed by variable rolling down as SH 35 turns inland to cross the Motu River. Easy gradients to return to the coast, then alternates between gentle undulations to traverse bays and rolling over headlands as the highway hugs the coast all the way to Waihau Bay. After Waihau Bay is a flat 5 km along Whangaparaoa Bay before a 1 km quite steep climb away from the coast. The last 38 km to Hicks Bay are inland with an occasional big hill interspersed by moderate rolls and gentle undulations.

**ATTRACTIONS:** The almost deserted highway passes picturesque bays, sheer headlands, quaint churches, tiny historic settlements, and sandy beaches. Apart from the last 40 km to Hicks Bay, SH 35 is never far from the coast and is considered by some to be one of the finest coastal cycling routes in the world. This is especially so during early summer when the pohutukawa blooms. While seemingly not lacking in numbers, the tree is endangered because there are so few young ones growing.

The coastal area is important to Maori culture, it is thought habitation in these parts began during the Toi period of about 11th century, which pre-dates the great migration fleet by 200 years. The Tainui, Arawa and other canoes are said to have made their first landfall at Whangaparaoa (Cape Runaway) from Hawaiki in about 1350 AD. This is the first place in New Zealand kumara were grown. Rejoin the coast at Hicks Bay, yet another tiny settlement in an idyllic setting.

### 8c. HICKS BAY - TOKOMARU BAY - GISBORNE.   182km

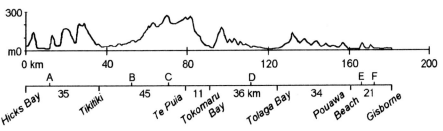

**SERVICES: HICKS BAY:** See previous section.
**A) TE ARAROA:** Alt 10m, pop 350. Store, takeaways, motor camp (6km north), hotel.
**TIKITIKI:** Alt 50m, pop 140. Hotel (also camping), bkpr hostel.
**B) RUATORIA:** Alt 60m, pop 1000. Food: All types of outlets except supermarket.
Accom: Motel; hotel. **C) TAKAPAU HILL:** Alt 280m picnic area.
**TE PUIA SPRINGS:** Alt 240m, pop 350. *i:* Main Road, ☎ 06 864 6853.
Store, takeaways, hotel (incl camping), motel.
**TOKOMARU BAY:** Alt 5m, pop 300. Store; tearooms; dairy/motor camp; pub; bkpr hostel; motel.
**D) ANAURA BAY:** Alt 5m. DoC camping (toilets, water, table), about 7km off SH 35.
**TOLAGA BAY:** Alt 5m, pop 550. Food: All types of outlets except supermarket.
Accom: Motor camp; bkpr hostel; motel 2; hotel.
**POUAWA BEACH:** picnic area. **TURIHAUA BEACH:** Informal camping (toilet, tables).
**F) TATAPOURI:** pub. **MAKORORI BEACH:** Picnic areas (toilet, table, shelter).
**H) OKITU:** Dairy **WAINUI:** Pop 500. Store, takeaways, restaurant, motel 2.
**GISBORNE:** See page 48.

**GRADIENTS:** Climbs variably steep for 2km on leaving Hick's Bay and similar descent to go over Pukeamaru Hill (140m). Then flat for 6 km to Araroa. before going up again. This is the first of three biggish hills that climb to 115m, 205m & 220m respectively, all in too few kilometres and ending with a long variable descent to Tikitiki. After Tikitiki, apart from a moderate river bluff, the gradients are easy for the 19 km to Ruatoria turn off. Rolls and undulates for 8 km, before a gradual 5½ km climb up Kopuora Valley. Becomes steeper before a short descent and up again variable for another 3 km to Takapau Hill at 280m. Down, some steep for 1½ km, then rolls up 7 km to Te Puia.
Note: There are an increasing number of logging trucks making their presence felt as the region's plantation forests reach maturity.

A last roll on leaving Te Puia, then a long 9 km descent to Tokomaru Bay, the decline easing near the bottom. A 200m climb out of Tokomaru Bay in 3 km goes to Parau Saddle, followed by a short roll and a 1 km steep descent. The next 28 km to Tolaga Bay have no serious hills with the last part being mostly flat. Continues similar leaving Tolaga Bay, but 3½ km after the wharf turn-off, SH 35 ascends for 3 km, becoming steeper as the summit (120m) nears. Long rolling hills follow to cross the watersheds of several rivers, before descending to rejoin the coast at Pouawa Beach. The 19 km to Gisborne are mostly flat along several beaches broken only by the occasional hill to traverse small headlands. The last 5 km from Wainui are inland.

**ATTRACTIONS:** Heading south from Hicks Bay, the highway covers a more distance inland than the previous stretch from Opotiki and so is less scenic as a consequence. Spectacular views from Pukeamaru Hill on the way from Hicks Bay. In the school grounds at Te Araroa is Te Waha o Rerekohu, one of NZ's oldest pohutukawa trees. It is believed to be over 600 years old. Leave SH 35 at Te Araroa to go to East Cape. At Tikitiki view the beautifully carved interior of St Mary's Church, considered one of the finest of Maori churches. Ruatoria is a rural service town has settled down in recent times after a period of wild molotov cocktail parties hosted by the local Rastafarians.

A short but steep detour on the way to Te Puia goes to Waipiro Bay, now almost deserted but once an important regional town until the highway went through. The Kerridge cinema chain had its origins here. Mt Hikurangi which becomes visible to the west and is the highest non-volcanic peak in the North Island at 1750m. Te Puia has a pleasant atmosphere with hot springs at the hotel.

Tokomaru Bay is yet another backwater settlement whose cluster of empty shops indicate the decline suffered since the freezing works closed, whose ruins are at nearby Waima Bay. After Anaura Bay comes Tolaga Bay, at 660m the wharf was the longest in the southern hemisphere and serviced the coastal shipping. Guess who the nearby Cook's Cove is named after? Pass several picturesque surfing beaches before arriving at Gisborne. See page 48.

# 9. GISBORNE - OPOTIKI - ROTORUA.

**ROUTE:**                                           SH 2/33/30
  9a) GISBORNE - MATAWAI - OPOTIKI          144 km
  9b) OPOTIKI - PAENGAROA - ROTORUA         152 km
Total                                              296 km

**ALTERNATIVE** 9b) KUTARERE - MATATA. SH 2 through Taneatua or the shorter, coast road through Ohope & Whakatane.
**LINK ROAD** 9b) i PAENGAROA - TAURANGA on SH 2.
**SIDE TRIP:** 9a) MATAWAI - MOTU.

## 9a. GISBORNE - MATAWAI - OPOTIKI. 144km

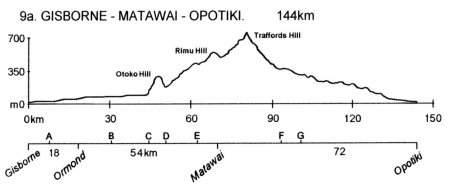

**SERVICES: GISBORNE:** See page 48-49. **A) WAERENGAAHIKA:** pub.
**ORMOND:** Store, pub. **B) TE KARAKA:** 1km off SH 2. Alt 45m, store, takeaways, pub.
**C) OTOKO:** Alt 50m, picnic area (at start of walkway). **D) OTOKO HALL** Alt 180m, picnic area.
**E) RAKAUROA:** Alt 460m, picnic area.
**MATAWAI:** Alt 540m, pop 200. Store, tearooms, motor camp (no cabins, key at the tearooms), hotel.
**F) MANGANUKU:** Alt 200m DoC camping (toilet, water) adj SH 2. **G) WAIRATA:** Alt 150m, picnic area.
**OPOTIKI:** Alt 5m, pop 6000. *i:* Cnr St John/Elliot Sts ☎ 07 315 8484. Food: All types of outlets.
Accom: Motor camp; bkpr hostel; motel 2; hotel 2.
Bicycle Shop: Marine & Cycle Centre, 90 Church St ☎ 07 315 5758.

**GRADIENTS:** Flat to begin with then follows Waipaoa River inland gently rising for many km. After Te Karaka gradients mostly uphill, steep climbs over Otoko & Rimu Hills on the way to Matawai. Another climb after Matawai before gradients ease around Trafford's Hill (725m). Descends sometimes quite steeply before entering Waioeka Gorge, with SH 2 twisting and turning its way down through the narrow bush clad hills on a mostly gradual fairly steep descent. Becomes flat as Opotiki nears.

**ATTRACTIONS:** Pass small settlements on the way to the interior. Otoko Walkway, adjacent to SH 2 is a short scenic track using an old rail corridor. Matawai is a quaint village from where a side road goes to Motu. The old coach road links with SH 35 at Opape on the coast, east of Opotiki. Being mostly unsealed through remote bush, it is popular with experienced mountain bikers.
   Magnificent scenery through Waioeka Gorge from Opato Bridge for much of the way to Opotiki. This is the largest scenic reserve in New Zealand with rugged terrain and splendid native flora and fauna. During the land wars Te Kooti used the area for a while as a base to raid nearby settlements.
   Opotiki was one of the first places in New Zealand to be settled, is now a small rural town. St Stephen's Church was built in 1865 by Rev Carl Sylvus Volkner, who came to a rather unpleasant end at the hands of Hauhau rebels, is buried in the church grounds. A local excursion goes to Hukutaia Domain where one of NZ's oldest trees, a puriri, is located. At one time it was used as a burial site.

**OPTIONS: SIDE TRIP:** MATAWAI - MOTU. Distance 13km. Sealed to Motu. This route leads to Old Motu Road, a remote and sometimes hilly scenic gravel track that arrives at the coast between Opape and Tirohanga (see page 42 for onward travel). No services.

## 9b. OPOTIKI - WHAKATANE - PAENGAROA - ROTORUA.   152km

**SERVICES: OPOTIKI:** See page 45 to Gisborne/Rotorua direct, or page 42 to East Cape.
**A) WAIOTAHI BEACH:** Alt 5m. Picnic area, tearooms, motor camp; bkpr hostel.
**KUTARERE:.** Leave SH 2 for the shorter route to Whakatane through Ohope.
**B) OHOPE:** Alt 5m, pop 2000. Food: All types of outlets except supermarket.
Accom: Motor camp 2; motel 6; hotel.
**WHAKATANE:** Alt 5m, pop 13,000. *i:* Boon St ☎ 07 308 6058.
Food: All types of outlets. Accom: Motor camp; bkpr hostel; motel 5; hotel 5.
Bicycle Shop: *Whakatane Cycle Centre, Boon St ☎ 07 308 8663.
*Spokes Cycle Centre, 109 The Strand ☎ 07 308 8501. **C) THORNTON:** Dairy, beach motor camp.
**MATATA:** Alt 10m. Dairy, tearooms, pub, motor camp/shop.
**D) PIKOWAI BEACH:** Domain camping (shelter, toilets, water, coin showers). **E) MANIATUTU:** shop.
**PAENGAROA:** (Junction SHs 2 & 33) Alt 30m, store, motel. **OTARAMARAE:** picnic area.
**OKERE FALLS:** Motor camp, picnic area. **F) MOUREA:** Store, tearooms, pub.
**ROTORUA:** See pages 27-28.

**GRADIENTS:** Flat leaving Opotiki, go right just after Kutarere for a short cut to Whakatane through Ohope. This road rolls a bit at first then becomes flat as it skirts around Ohiwa Harbour to Ohope Beach. Travel parallel to the beach, then take an abrupt steep climb away from Ohope. On reaching the top it rolls before a moderate quite steep descent to Whakatane.
   Flat on leaving Whakatane until the end of Kohioawa Beach, then rolls and undulates to Paengaroa. Go left to Rotorua. Climbs gently at first, becoming variable uphill. 2 km after entering the pine plantation SH 33 descends for 1 km before resuming up again for 4 km. It then rolls and meanders along for a while before a final 2½ km variable climb to what is the stiff upper lip of the central volcanic plateau. A 1 km descent to Okere Falls then mostly easy gradients from there to Rotorua except a small hill at Okawa Bay.

**ATTRACTIONS:** Ohope Beach is a popular holiday resort. Offshore the smouldering volcanic White Island dominates the scene from most parts of the Bay of Plenty. Whakatane has a pleasant air to it, seasonal dolphin swimming goes from here as well as other fishy related sports. The Bay of Plenty and Rotorua areas are of importance to the Arawa Tribe, being settled by descendants of the Arawa canoe of the great fleet, whose final resting place is considered to be at Maketu.

**OPTIONS: ALTERNATIVE:** KUTARERE - AWAKERI - MATATA. Distance 58 km. By-passes the "big" city of Whakatane but is 8 km longer. Mostly flat except for rolling hills between Kutarere and Tamatea. KUTARERE: See above. TANEATUA: Store. AWAKERI: Dairy, takeaways, motor camp. EDGECUMBE: Store, dairy, takeaways, pub.

**LINK ROAD i** PAENGAROA - TAURANGA. Distance: 36 km. Rolls and undulates.
Te Puke is one of the main kiwifruit fruit growing regions. At the western end of Bay of Plenty is Tauranga, a bustling port and city with nearby Mount Maunganui a popular kiwi holiday resort, especially with drunken louts at New Year!
**PAENGAROA:** Alt 30m, store, motel. **RANGIURU:** picnic area.
**TE PUKE:** Pop 5200. *i:* Jellico St. ☎ 07 573 9172. Food: All types of outlets.
Accom: Motor camp; bkpr hostel; motel. Bicycle Shop: *AttrillsCycles, 124 Jellico St ☎ 07 573 7019.
**PAPAMOA:** Alt 10m pop 400. Store, motor camp 2; motel.
**MT MAUNGANUI:** Alt 5m, pop 15,000. *i:* Salisbury Ave ☎ 07 575 5099.
Food: All types of outlets. Accom: Motor camp 4; bkpr hostel 2; motel 8; hotel 1.
TAURANGA: See page 25.

# 10. ROTORUA - LAKE WAIKAREMOANA - WAIROA.

**ROUTE:** ROTORUA - WAIROA on SH 38.    Distance: 211 km

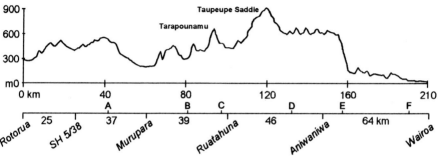

**SERVICES: ROTORUA:** See pages 27-28. **A) KAINGAROA FOREST:** Alt 545m, picnic area.
**MURUPARA:** Alt 185m, pop 3000. *i:* DoC Visitor Centre, SH 38, ☎ 07 366 1080.
Food: Store, takeaways. Accom: The motor camp may have closed, motel, hotel.
**B) TE WHAITI:** Motel, picnic area. **C) MIMIHA BRIDGE:** Alt 350m, informal camping, adj SH 38.
**RUATAHUNA:** Alt 425m, store, pub. **TAUPEUPE SADDLE:** Alt 919m, picnic area (shelter).
**D) HOPURUAHINE LANDING:** DoC camping (toilets, water, table) short way off SH 38.
**MOKAU LANDING:** Alt 590m, DoC camping (toilets, water, table).
**ANIWANIWA:** Alt 590m. *i:* DoC Visitor Centre ☎ 06 837 3803. DoC camping (toilets, water, table).
**WAIKAREMOANA:** Alt 590m. Store/motor camp/motel.
**ROSIE BAY:** picnic area (toilet, table). **E) TUAI:** Alt 300m, Store, tearooms, motor camp.
**F) FRASERTOWN:** Alt 15, pop 500. Dairy/takeaways, pub. **WAIROA:** See page 49.

**GRADIENTS:** Rolls and undulates up out of Rotorua to SH 5/38 junction, then becomes gentle rolling as the road passes through Kaingaroa Forest. A long gradual 20 km descent begins gentle but becoming steeper, then levelling out shortly before Murupara. Cross the broad Whirinaki Valley before heading back into the hills, this time with a vengeance. Apart from flattish sections around Te Whaiti and Ruatahuna, it is a narrow, tortuous but scenic road for much of the way to Lake Waikaremoana. Gravel starts at Te Whaiti and ends at Tuai, apart from a section of tar-seal around Ruatahuna.

After Ruatahuna there is a 9 km climb to Taupeupe Saddle (919m) then a descent for 12 km to Hopuruahine Landing at Lake Waikaremoana. SH 38 then rolls steeply at times alongside the lake to the spillway. A quite steep descent from there for 8½ km to Piripaua Power Station (150m), before levelling out. Alternates between rolls and undulations until 12 km before Frasertown when the hills gradually fall away for the last time and gradients ease. The last few km into Wairoa are almost flat.

**ATTRACTIONS:** After passing through the vast Kaingaroa Forest plantation, arrive at the small logging settlement of Murupara, on the Rangitaiki River, after which things get scenic and rugged. 15 km up a side road from Te Whaiti is the forestry settlement of MINGINUI: (DoC camping) set deep in the Whirinaki Forest Park around which are a few mountain biking oportunities. After passing through several tiny settlements arrive at the rugged Te Urewera National Park.

The jewel of the park is Lake Waikaremoana (Sea of Rippling Water). Being up to 250m deep it was formed about 2,000 years ago when a giant slip blocked Taheke River. The distinctive Panekiri Bluff is a prominent landmark. There are numerous walks in and around the park with the popular lake circuit being a DoC Great Walk of several days. There are the usual watery activities on the lake. This is the home of the Tuhoe Tribe or "children of the mist", who for a long time lived completely cut off from the outside world. After leaving the park pass through an impressive gorge and enter pastoral country for the last part to Wairoa.

# 11. GISBORNE - WAIROA - NAPIER.

| **ROUTE:** | SH 2 | SH 36 |
|---|---|---|
| 11a) GISBORNE - WAIROA | 99 km | 102 km |
| 11b) WAIROA - NAPIER | 118 km | |
| Total | 217 km | |

**ALTERNATIVE** 11a) GISBORNE - WAIROA. The busier SH 2 or more challenging SH 36.
**SIDE TRIP** 11a) NUHAKA - MAHIA PENINSULA.

## 11a. GISBORNE - MORERE - WAIROA.    99km

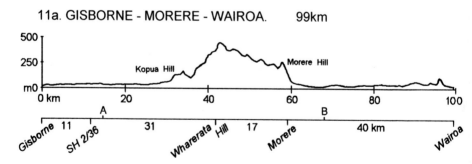

**SERVICES: GISBORNE:** Alt 5m, pop 30,000. *i:* 209 Grey St ☎ 06 868 6139.
Food: All types of outlets. Accom: Motor camp 2; hostel (bkpr 2, YHA 1); motel 15; hotel 3.
Transport:  Bus & shuttle to/from Opotiki, Napier & Hicks Bay.
Bicycle Shop: *City Cycles, 103 Wainui Rd ☎ 06 867 3677. *Gisborne Cycles, 155 Grey St ☎ 06 867 6249. *Main Trax Cycles, Cnr Gladstone/Roebuck Rds ☎ 06 867 4571.

**A) MANUTUKE:** Store. **WHARERATA HILL:** Alt 488m, picnic area (table).
**MORERE:** Alt 40m, pop 100. Store, tearooms, pub, motor camp, bkpr hostel (seasonal).
**B) NUHAKA:** Alt 20m, store/takeaways.
**WAIROA:** Altitude 5m, pop 5500. *i:* Cnr SH 2/Queen St ☎ 06 838 7440.
Food: All types of outlets. Accom: Motor camp; bkpr hostel 2 (one is 13km S); motel 2; hotel 3.
Transport: Bus & shuttle to/from Lake Waikaremoana, Napier & Gisborne.

**GRADIENTS:** Mostly flat from Gisborne for the first 30 km then a 4½ km fairly steep ascent up Kopua Hill (120m) followed by a moderate 3 km descent. Go up variably steep for 8 km to the top of Wharerata Hill (488m) and a rolling, stepped downhill for 12½ km. A short climb to Morere Hill (280m). Is followed by a 4 km quite steep descent to Morere village. Gentle downhill for the 8 km to Nuhaka then mostly flat as SH 2 turns west and runs parallel to the eastern end of Hawke Bay except for a short steep hill just before Wairoa.

**ATTRACTIONS:** Gisborne is the biggest city in the Poverty Bay region, in recent years a reputable vine and fruit growing industry has developed. It is here in Oct 1769 that Captain Cook made the first known landing in New Zealand of a European. The Cook Memorial on Kaiti Beach records the event. At nearby Matawhero in 1868 Te Kooti murdered many local Maori & European in what was called the Poverty Bay Massacre, the church being the only building he spared, is still standing. Gisborne is the gateway to East Cape and claims to be the first city in the world to see the sun, if it isn't cloudy.
  Morere has hot springs and is a pleasant spot after the ascent of Wharerata Hill, which has spectacular views over Poverty Bay and beyond Gisborne from Wharerata look-out. A side trip goes from Nuhaka to Opoutama Beach and the Mahia Peninsula. On the way to Wairoa, pass Whakaki Lagoon, a notable feeding ground for migratory birds.
  Wairoa is the gateway to Lake Waikaremoana and Te Urewera National Park. It is the only sizeable town between Gisborne and Napier and sits astride of Wairoa River. This river should not be confused with Wairoa River at Dargaville; Wairoa River at Clevedon; Wairoa River and Pa near Tauranga; Wairua River near Whangarei or Wairau River at Blenheim. Nor is it to be mistaken for Wairau Lagoon, Wairau Valley, Wairau Pa, Wairau Bar (& grill), Wairau Arm (& Leg) or Wairau Incident!

**OPTIONS: ALTERNATIVE** GISBORNE - WAIROA - on SH 36. Distance: 102 km.
This route is 3 km longer than SH 2, is much hillier but has little traffic. The highway alternates between flattish stretches and long steep ascents and descents. The route has some interesting sights, from and to, such places as Te Reiinga Falls, Doneraille Park and Gentle Annie Hill.
**GENTLE ANNIE:** Alt 304m, picnic area. **WAERENGAOKURI:** store.
**DONERAILLE PARK:** Alt 240m, domain camping (toilet, water) down steep side road.
**TINIROTO:** Alt 260m, pop 200, pub. **MARUMARU:** pub.
**FRASERTOWN:** Alt 15, pop 500. Dairy/takeaways, pub. **WAIROA:** see above.

**SIDE TRIP:** NUHAKA - MAHIA PENINSULA at the northern end of Hawkes Bay. Go 16 km from Nuhaka on a quiet, narrow but sealed road to MAHIA BEACH (motor camp with small shop/tearooms), a local holiday resort. Moderately hilly at first from Nuhaka but flat after OPOUTAMA BEACH (motor camp has closed). It is possible to continue further on a scenic road and passing isolated beaches.

## 11b. WAIROA - LAKE TUTIRA - NAPIER.   118km

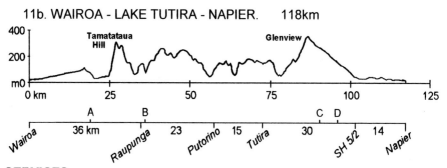

**SERVICES: WAIROA:** See page 49. **A) WAIHUA BEACH:** picnic area.
**TAUMATATAUA HILL:** picnic area. **RAUPUNGA:** Alt 100m, pop 300, picnic area.
**B) MOHAKA RIVER:** Alt 40m, picnic area (table).
**KOTEMAORI:** (3km NE) bkpr farm hostel. **PUTORINO:** Alt 85m, pop 300, dairy, pub.
**LAKE TUTIRA:** Alt 160m, DoC camping (toilets, water, table, shelter) adj SH 2, store.
**GLENVIEW:** Alt 340m, bkpr hostel, 2km off SH 2.
**C) WHITE PINE:** Alt 280m, picnic area. **D) TANGOIO:** Alt 75m, picnic area.
**NAPIER:** Alt 5m, pop 51,000. *i:* 100 Marine Pde ☎ 06 834 1911.
Food: All types of outlets. Accom: Motor camp 2; hostel (bkpkr 4, YHA 1); motel lots; hotel many.
Transport: Bus & shuttles to/from Wellington, Gisborne & Taupo.
Bicycle shop: *Marewa Cycles, Kennedy Rd ☎ 06 845 9243. *Napier Kart & Cycle Centre, 1 Clive Sq,
☎ 06 835 9528. *Pedal Power, 340 Gloucester St, Taradale ☎ 06 844 9771. Not a complete list.

**GRADIENTS:** SH 2 starts quite tame for most of the first 25 km from Wairoa then the hills start with
a 180m ascent in 2 km, followed by a steep roll to the top of Taumatataua Hill (250m). Down in two
leaps and a bound to Mohaka River, up steep to Raupunga and back down again to Mohaka Gorge.
Pass under the viaduct as you climb once more out of the gorge. There are two more gorges of Waikari
and Matahorua to traverse before Lake Tutira and have considerable elevation loss/gain in short
distances, like steep. Otherwise the highway rolls and undulates. Busy with large trucks.
   A gentle climb beings from Lake Tutira before plunging 130m in 1½ km to level out at Waikoau River.
Almost flat before a steep 1 km climb and a short descent to go through the hairpin bends of Devil's
Elbow, then resumes a skyward direction of 200m in 3 km before leveling out at 340m. Now follows a
variable 15 km descent, the middle bit around White Pine and Tangoio Scenic Reserves being the
steepest. SH 2 ends as it began, the last 19 km into Napier are flat, running parallel to the coastline.

**ATTRACTIONS:** For Wairoa see page 49. Pass under and marvel at the Mohaka Viaduct, a piece
of modern engineering 40 km from Wairoa. At 100m above the river it is the highest in New Zealand.
It will make a excellent cycle trail when the railway line eventually closes! Lake Tutira has a wildlife
refuge and is one of the highlights of the journey from Wairoa. On the way to Napier pass the aptly
named Devil's Elbow and the scenic reserves of Tangoio & White Pine.
   Hawke Bay has the twin centres of Hastings & Napier and is an important horticultural area with wine
tours and seasonal orchard work. The statue Pania of the Reef went walk-about and mysteriously
disappeared one dark night in October 2005. She was found a few days later having a quiet sleep in
someone's shed! Napier was devastated by an earthquake in 1931 and have an earthquake museum
that tells you all about it. Napier was rebuilt using an "art-deco" architectural style that gives the city a
special character. Nearby at Cape Kidnappers is reputedly the world's only mainland gannet colony.
Te Mata Peak near Havelock North is worth the climb for views of the Bay area.

**HIGHLIGHTS** (not in any order of preference):

Wellington City & Regional Parks
Art Deco of Napier
Gannet Colony at Cape Kidnappers
Martinborough wine region
Mt Bruce Wildlife Park

Manawatu Gorge
Tararua and Ruahine Forest Parks
Woolly jumpers at Norsewood
Beaches on the Wairarapa Coast
Pongaroa, Porangahau & peace of SH 52

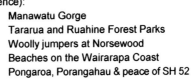

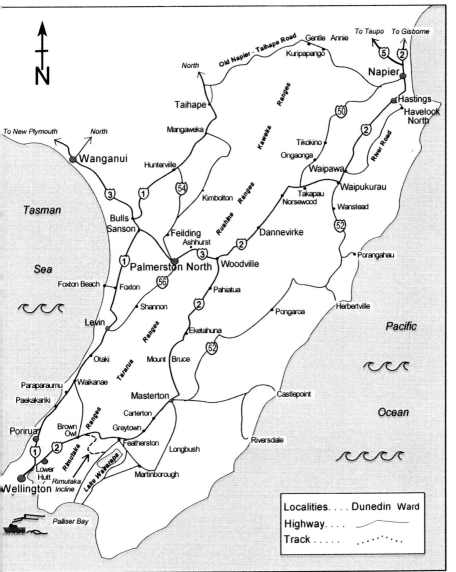

Localities. . . . Dunedin Ward
Highway. . . .
Track . . . . .

# 12. TAUPO - NAPIER.

**ROUTE:** NAPIER - TAUPO on SH 5.  Distance:  143 km

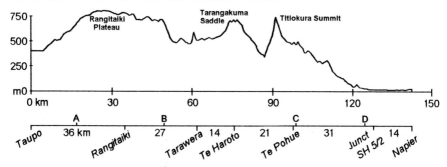

**SERVICES: TAUPO:** See page 29. **A) OPEPE RESERVE:** Alt 730m, picnic area.
**RANGITAIKI:** Alt 680m, motel/motor camp (also shop, tearooms), (then 5 km to) pub.
**B) FALLS LOOKOUT:** Alt 700m, picnic area.
**TARAWERA:** Alt 500m. pub/tearooms/motor camp (no kitchen or cabins).
**TE HAROTO:** Alt 700m tearooms. **TE POHUE:** Alt 480m hotel. **C) ESK FOREST:** picnic area (shelter).
**D) ESKDALE:** Motor camp, (no cabins). **NAPIER:** See page 50 or 53.

**GRADIENTS:** Three major saddles and numerous smaller hills must be crossed before arriving at Hawke Bay. Elevation gain/loss is many metres in (too?) few kilometres.
   A variable climb from Lake Taupo goes to the Kaingaroa Plateau (765m), then mostly easy terrain until after Rangitaiki. Between the Falls Lookout and Te Pohue, SH 5 becomes hilly with some long steep descents and ascents, particularly down from the falls lookout, up to Tarangakuma Saddle (710m) down to Mohaka River (315m) up to Titiokura Summit (720m) and down again  to Te Pohue (460m). After Dillons Hill is a long variable descent going all the way to Eskdale where the highway levels out. Flat on joining SH 2 for the last 14km into Napier.

**ATTRACTIONS:** After leaving Lake Taupo behind comes Opepe Reserve, adjacent to SH 5, it is a pleasant spot, completely out of keeping with the bloody encounter that took place here last century. Comes complete with a cemetery of the victims. Go from the high pumice plains of the central plateau to the low coastal plains around Napier. In between traverse high saddles and deep narrow river gorges. Pass waterfalls, hot springs and small settlements; native bush and pine plantations; historic and scenic reserves; conservation areas, big logging trucks and some fascinating woolly sheep with curly bits on the end. Orchards and vineyards start to appear as Napier nears.

# 13. NAPIER - WOODVILLE - WELLINGTON.

## ROUTE:

| | SH 2 |
|---|---|
| 13a) NAPIER - WOODVILLE | 152 km |
| 13b) WOODVILLE - WELLINGTON | 181 km* |
| Total | 333 km |

* Add 8 km if using Rimutaka Incline.

_TERNATIVE 13a) i HASTINGS/NAPIER - TAKAPAU on SH 2 or SH 50 through Tikokino (Page 54).
ii HASTINGS/NAPIER - WAIPAWA on SH 2 or through Havelock North (Page 54).
iii WAIPUKURAU - MASTERTON on SH 2 or SH 52 through Pongaroa (Page 54).
13b) i MASTERTON - FEATHERSTON on SH 2 or through Martinborough (page 56).
ii FEATHERSTON - KAITOKE on SH 2 or Rimutaka Incline (page 57).
NK ROAD 13a) NAPIER - GENTLE ANNIE - TAIHAPE. On Old Napier - Taihape Road (Page 55).
13b) WOODVILLE - PALMERSTON NORTH on SH 3. (Page 61).
DE TRIP 13b) i MASTERTON - MT HOLDSWORTH (Page 57).
ii MASTERTON - CASTLEPOINT & RIVERSDALE BEACHES (Page 57).

## 13a. NAPIER - HASTINGS - WOODVILLE. 152km

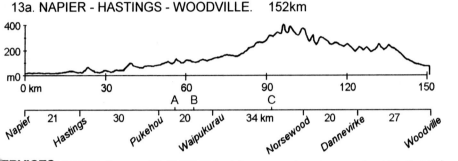

**ERVICES: NAPIER:** See page 50. **CLIVE:** Dairy, takeaways, pub, motor camp (no cabins); motel.
**ASTINGS:** Alt 20m, pop 37,000. *i:* Russell St N ☎ 06 878 5526. Food: All types of outlets.
:com: Motor camp 2; bkpr hostel 3; motel 13; hotel 5.
cycle Shop: *The Hub, 1021 Heretaunga St W ☎ 06 876 9363.
JKEHOU: Alt 80m, store. **A) OTANE:** (1 km off SH 2) pub.
WAIPAWA: Alt 140m, pop 1800. Food: All types of outlets. Accom: Motor camp (no cabins); motel.
cycle Shop: Booker Cycles, 57 Ruataniwha St ☎ 06 858 9377.
AIPUKURAU: Alt 140m, pop 4500. *i:* Railway Esplanade ☎ 06 858 6488. Food: All types of outlets.
:com: Motor camp; bkpr hostel 2 (one is 22 km S on Route 52); motel 2; hotel 2.
TAKAPAU: 2 km off SH 2. Alt 240m, store, takeaways, hotel.
ORSEWOOD: Alt 380m, pop 350. Store, tearooms, domain camping (toilets, water) 4 km N of town;
ahive bkpr cabin; hotel.
ANNEVIRKE: Alt 200m, pop 6000. *i:* 156 High St ☎ 06 374 8343. Food: All types of outlets.
:com: Motor camp; motel 2; hotel 3.
OODVILLE: Alt 95m, pop 1800. *i:* 7 Vogel St ☎ 06 376 5742.
od: All types of outlets except supermarket. Accom: Domain camping (no kitchen, cabins or lounge);
tel 2; hotel. Transport: Bus & shuttles to/from Wellington, Wanganui & Napier.

**RADIENTS:** Note: Consider using the Middle Road through Havelock North to Waipawa as SH 2
n be busy. Flat around Napier and Hastings then alternates between undulations and rolling hills but
thing too extreme with the first hill just after Pakipaki. Turn west at Waipukerau and start a steady
0m climb across the Takapau Plains. Some steep roller coaster dips and climbs to cross rivers begin
Manawatu River just before Norsewood, easing to undulations just before Dannevirke. Alternates
tween flat to rolling all the way from Dannevirke to Woodville with just the occasional small hill.

**ATTRACTIONS:** Central Hawke Bay has the twin centres of Hastings & Napier and is an important horticultural area with wine tours and seasonal orchard work. In 1931 Napier was devastated by a serious earthquake and they have an earthquake museum that tells you all about it. Napier was rebuilt using an architectural style commonly known as art-deco which gives the city a special character. Nearby at Cape Kidnappers is reputedly the world's only mainland gannet colony. Te Mata Peak near Havelock North is worth the climb for views of the Bay area.

Heading south, Norsewood and Dannevirke will be of interest to cycling Vikings, being founded last century by Scandinavian migrants. Norsewood is famous for high quality woollen garments made at the Norsewear mill, complete with a factory shop. Like many parts of the North Island, European settlement of the region started by turning the native forest into farmland.

To the west, the Ruahine and Tararua Mountains are separated only by the narrow Manawatu Gorge. The Manawatu River is unusual in that it starts on the eastern slopes of the Ruahine Mountains, then turns west to go through the gorge. Woodville is on the junction of SH2 and 3.

**OPTIONS: ALTERNATIVE i** NAPIER - TIKOKINO - TAKAPAU on SH 50. Distance: 84 km.
9 km shorter than SH 2 through Hastings with less traffic.

Mostly flat to undulating upstream from Napier to Maraekakaho, after which SH 50 leaves Ngaruroro River with a minor hill. A long variable climb alongside Maraekakaho River before eases to rolling around Glenlyon at 365m. This is followed by a variable steep descent along Mangaonuku Stream to Richardson Bridge. Undulates and rolls for the last leg with a flattish bit round Waipawa River
ONGAONGA: Alt 200m, store, pub. TIKOKINO: Alt 235m, store, pub.
FERNHILL: Alt 20m All types of food outlets. NAPIER: See above.

**ALTERNATIVE ii** NAPIER/HASTINGS - HAVELOCK NORTH - WAIPAWA. This route is much quieter than SH 2 and bypasses central Hastings.

Leave SH 2 near Clive going to Havelock North, take Middle Road and climb to about 100m with the Kaokaoroa Hills to the east. After the variable descent follow Tukituki River to Waipawa, the road rolls and undulates all the way.
HAVELOCK NORTH: Pop 8800. Food: All types of outlets. Accom: Motor camp; motel; hotel. Bicycle Shop: Revolution Bikes, 17 Napier Road ☎ 06 877 8477. Nearby is the distinctive Te Mata Peak with spectacular views from the top, where hang-gliders hang out. To the east are a couple of seaside resorts, Waimarama (tearooms, motor camp) & Ocean Beach.
PATANGATA (pub). Rejoin SH 2 at Waipawa.

**ALTERNATIVE iii** WAIPUKURAU - PONGAROA - MASTERTON on SH 52. Distance: 197 km.
WAIPUKURAU: See above. WANSTEAD: pub, bkpr farm hostel. PORANGAHAU: Dairy, hostel, hotel.
PORANGAHAU BEACH: (7 flat km off SH 52) Motor camp (small shop), lodge.
HERBERTVILLE: 12 km off SH 52. Motor camp (no cabins); pub.
PONGAROA: Store, dairy, bkpr farm hostel (9½ km SW adj SH 52); pub. MASTERTON: See below.

Much less traffic than SH 2 on a scenic back country road. Occasional long steepish hill to traverse and some gravel between Wimbledon (Herbertville turn-off) and Porangahau. This can be used with other roads as an alternative to SH 2 between Featherston and Hastings/Napier.

Near Porangahau is the world's longest place name. Get your lips around this one!
Taumatawhakatangihangakoauauotamatea(turipukakapimaungahoronuku)pokaiwhenuakitanatahu. Which means "the place where Tamatea, (the man with the big knees, who slid climbed and swallowed mountains) who travelled over the land, played his flute to his loved one". Or so they say!

Pongaroa was the birthplace of Professor Maurice Wilkins, one of the discoverers of the DNA double helix. Also near Pongroa is the scenic Waihi Falls.

**INK ROAD:** NAPIER - GENTLE ANNIE - TAIHAPE. On the Old Napier - Taihape Road.

Distance: Taihape - Kuripapango 77km, Kuripapango - Napier 73 km.

It is better to go from Taihape to Napier but I didn't have room for this in that region! It is more suited for mountain bikers as there is about 45 km of gravel, rough in places and some parts like riding on marbles. Very quiet but beware logging trucks and stock trucks around the Napier Sales days. Get the inland Patea Heritage Trails brochure of Hawke's Bay and Rangitikei Districts if they're still available.

The road follows an ancient Maori trail and there are several long steep climb and descents with the highest point reaching 960m as the road traverses the Kaweka Range. In the vicinity of Gentle Annie and Kuripapango the road crosses a major fault line (beware roads called "Gentle Annie"!). This is where the Pacific and Indian continental plates meet and results in a dramatic landscape as they slide past each other. There is a long steep climb to leave Hawke Bay with splendid views from the top at the panorama viewpoint. Remote and hard work but scenic.

Near the site of a hotel burnt down in 1901 is. . . .

KURIPAPANGO: DoC camping (toilet, table, water). See the historic Springvale suspension bridge at

RANGITIKEI RIVER: Informal camping. Use the Inland Patea Heritage Trails brochure.

## 13b WOODVILLE - MASTERTON - WELLINGTON.  181km

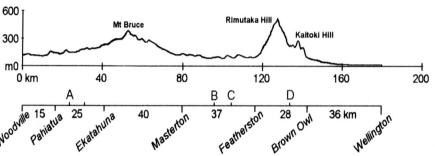

SERVICES: **WOODVILLE:** Alt 95m, pop 1800. *i:* 7 Vogel St ☎ 06 376 5742.
Food: All types of outlets except supermarket. Accom: Domain camping (no kitchen, cabins or lounge); hotel 2; hotel. Transport: Bus & shuttles to/from Wellington, Wanganui & Napier.

**PAHIATUA:** Alt 110m, pop 2000. Food: All types of outlets except supermarket. Accom: Motor camp (no cabins); motel 2; hotel. **A) HAMUA:** Alt 210m, picnic area.

**EKETAHUNA:** Alt 230m, pop 600. Food: All types of outlets except supermarket.
Accom: Domain motor camp; hotel. **MT BRUCE:** Alt 300m, tearooms, bird sanctuary, picnic area.

**MASTERTON:** Alt 120m, pop 18,000. *i:* Queen Elizabeth Park, 5 Dixon St ☎ 06 378 7373.
Food: All types of outlets. Accom: Motor camp; motel 6; hotel 2.
Transport: Train to/from Wellington stop operating at the end of September. Buses to/from Wellington, Palmerston North & Napier.
Bicycle Shop: *Lambert Cycles, Lincoln Rd ☎ 06 378 8844. *Happy Valley Cycling Centre, 8 Church St ☎ 06 377 1726. *A & D Cycles, 288 Queen St ☎ 06 377 3366.

**B) CARTERTON:** Alt 70m, pop 6500. Food: All types of outlets. Accom: Motor camp; motel; hotel.
Bicycle Shop: Kemp Goodwin, 52-58 High St ☎ 06 379 8294.

**C) GREYTOWN:** Alt 50m, pop 1800. Food: All types of outlets except supermarket.
Accom: Domain motor camp (no cabins); motel; hotel 2. **TAUHERENIKAU:** Pub.

**FEATHERSTON:** Alt 40m, pop 2500. *i:* The Courthouse, Fitzherbert St ☎ 06 308 8051.
Food: All types of outlets except supermarket. Accom: Motel; hotel.
**ABBOTT'S CREEK:** picnic area. **RIMUTAKA HILL:** Alt 555m, tearooms, toilets.
**D) KAITOKE:** Alt 220m, DoC style camping (water, toilet, table) in regional park.
**BROWN OWL:** Alt 60m, dairy, takeaways. **WELLINGTON:** See next section.

# GRADIENTS: Undulates for most of the way from Woodville until a moderate 2 km ascent of Mt

Bruce (365m), which is followed by a similar 2 km descent to Ruamahanga River. Then rolling hills for
5 km before a gradual descent of the Opaki Plain to Masterton.

Flat to undulating between Masterton and Featherston. Then starts a gradual 3½ km climb, followed
by sometimes quite steep and twisting 7½ km variable ascent of Rimutaka Hill (555m). Winds can be
strong up here! After the summit is a moderate 6½ km descent on a narrow, winding road, becoming
flatter before Kaitoke. After Kaitoke SH 2 becomes rolling, sometimes quite steep, with a 1 km steep
climb to the top of Kaitoke Hill (275m) on the way passing the Rimutaka Incline turn-off. 3 km steep and
twisting descent to Mangaroa River is followed by rolling terrain and ending with a short steep drop to
Brown Owl. The last part is a gentle descent of the Hutt Valley and flat ride alongside Wellington
Habour that brings one into the City.

A suburban train goes between Wellington and Masterton for those afraid of the big bad hill!

# ATTRACTIONS: At the northern end of the Tararua Ranges is the impressive Manawatu Gorge

above which can be seen one of NZ's first windfarms. Pahiatua is known for its broad main street, while
Eketahuna is most notable for being a place on the way to somewhere else. Adjacent to SH 2, between
Eketahuna and Masterton is Mt Bruce, a DoC National Wildlife Centre with breeding programmes for
several endangered native birds, open to the public. Many of the towns were established to clear the
dense 70 Mile Bush that stretched from Manawatu to Hawke Bay.

Masterton, Carterton, Greytown and Featherston straddle SH 2 and all service the surrounding
communities. The region is also becoming an important horticultural area. Masterton is the main centre
of the Wairarapa region. To the west a number of tramping tracks provide access to the rugged Tararua
Ranges such as Mt Holdsworth. About 11km SE of Carterton is Stonehenge Aotearoa, a specially built
structure that combines ancient technologies: the obelisk, developed by the Mesopotamians (c. 6000
BC); stone circles found throughout Europe (c 3000 BC); and a Polynesian star compass which was
developed in south-east Asia (c. 3000 BC), check for opening times.

Featherston has a fell railway museum with stuff left over from the Rimutaka Incline, now a cycle and
tramping trail going from Featherston to Kaitoke, see alternative below. Over Rimutaka Hill is the
Kaitoke Regional Park with walking and rafting possibilities. Some scenes in the Lord of the Rings films
were shot on location here. Enter the Hutt Valley with Wellington Harbour and city beyond.

# OPTIONS: ALTERNATIVE i MASTERTON - MARTINBOROUGH - FEATHERSTON. Head south

from Masterton through Gladstone and Longbush to Martinborough for an alternative to SH 2. New
Zealand's first sheep station was established at Martinborough, 18 km SE of Featherston, which is now
becoming famous as a wine growing region. The town's streets are laid out in the form of a Union Jack.
**MARTINBOROUGH:** Pop 1500. Food: All types of outlets except supermarket.
Accom: Domain camping (no cabins); motel; hotel.

Or continue south to the large but shallow Lake Wairarapa, an important wetlands and waterfowl area.
At the North Island's southern tip is the remote Cape Palliser with its seal colony and pinnacles.
PIRINOA (Store), LAKE FERRY (motor camp; hotel). Care is needed after heavy rain.

**ALTERNATIVE ii** FEATHERSTON - RIMUTAKA INCLINE - KAITOKE. Distance: 28 km.
This is about 8 km longer than SH 2, avoids all the traffic over Rimutaka Hill and the zenith is 200m lower. Access at Cross Creek from Western Lake Road, 10 km from Featherston and exit north side of Kaitoke Hill. It follows the route of an old mountain railway and includes tunnels, bridges, cuttings, embankments and washouts. More suitable for mountain and cross bikes with little weight
This Wairarapa side is steeper with an incline of 1:15. Care is needed on this side as it can be difficult and narrow in places, specially at the beginning and Siberia Washout area. A train was blown off the tracks here in 1880! Pass through the 580m long Summit Tunnel (torch recommended) and emerge at the Summit (350m). Travel down on a mostly well formed gravel surface through the Pakuratahi Forest. The pine plantation has been almost completely cleared on the Wellington side.
Informal camping (toilet, water) at Cross Creek, Summit (also shelter) and Ladle Bend. There is a brochure on the Rimutaka Incline available

**SIDE TRIP i** MT HOLDSWORTH is one of the main access points to the Tararua Ranges, with several walks and longer tramps in the area. DoC camping (toilets, water, tables) and Field Centre.
**SIDE TRIP ii** MASTERTON - CASTLEPOINT & RIVERSDALE BEACHES. 69 km and 56 km respectively. These are holiday resorts on the remote and rugged Wairarapa Coast. TINUI: hotel. CASTLEPOINT: Store, motor camp, motel, hotel. RIVERSDALE: Store, motor camp (no cabins),

# 4. WELLINGTON.

**ATTRACTIONS:** Wellington is the world's most southern capital city, set in one of the more picturesque locations. To get an eyeful, the Cable Car top station has panoramic views of the city and Port Nicolson. It also provides access to the Botanic Gardens and Carter Observatory. Mount Victoria offers more spectacular views from a different angle.
Wellington has been the Capital since the title was bestowed in 1864 following brief stints at Russell and Auckland. There are few historic attractions to go and have nosey round, such as Parliament building; St Paul's Church; Katherine Mansfield birthplace and the odd wooden shack. The original Waitangi Treaty document (or one of them) is housed in the National Archives. Te Papa, the new Museum of New Zealand has been very popular since opening in 1998 but some call it a glorified fun park. Additionally there are several art galleries & museums, including an interesting Maritime Museum (if you're interested in maritime).
As expected in a city the size of Wellington, there is plenty of night life with an array of clubs, pubs, cafés and restaurants. The widely acclaimed New Zealand International Festival of the Arts is held here biennially in March with performers participating from throughout the world, hence "International".
is a hilly city and has a reputation for being windy. This may be more due to the parliamentary activities but could also refer to the weather. The city has a number of walks in, around and through it and there are several tours from the city. A couple of them are: to Makara Beach to the west and to Pencarrow Head through Petone and Eastbourne, on the eastern side of Wellington Harbour.
A cycle/walking track has been developed along the Hutt River between the Estuary Bridge, at the eastern end of the Esplanade (Lower Hutt) and Brown Owl (Upper Hutt), 25 km away, with several access points en route. Some parts are gravel and gates may be locked. Hopes are to eventually link with the Rimutaka Incline. A track traversing the length of the Wellington region's coastline is in the development stage with a long term aim to join with the Hutt River Trail. The area around Wellington is popular amongst mountain bikers with the famous Kennet brothers being based here and have developed a mountain biking park at Makara. Karapoti up the Akatarawa Valley between Brown Owl and Waikanae is another popular area for mountain biking.

**SERVICES: WELLINGTON:** Altitude 5m, population: 330,000. ☎ toll call prefix is 04.
*i:* Civic Square, 101 Wakefield St ☎ 801 4000. Food: Many of all types of outlets.
Accommodation: Motor camp none; hostel (bkpr 6, YHA 1); motel multitudes; hotel many.
Transport: Trains to/from Auckland stop operating at the end of September. Suburban train to/from
Paraparaumu, Upper Hutt & Masterton. Bus & shuttles to/from almost everywhere south of Auckland.
Bicycle Shops: CENTRAL: *On Yer bike, 181 Vivian St ☎ 04 384 8480.
*Penny Farthing, 89 Courntney Pl., ☎ 385 2279.
**PORIRUA:** Food: All types of food outlets. Accom: Motor camp; motel 2; hotel.
Bicycle Shops: Porirua Cycle Centre, 81 Kenepuru Dr ☎ 237 4085.
**LOWER HUTT:** *i:* Queensgate Shopping Centre ☎ 566 7218.
Food: All types of outlets. Accom: Motor camp; motel 11; hotel 6.
Bicycle Shops: *On Yer bike, 418 High St ☎ 04 566 8773. *VIC Cycles, 461 High St ☎ 569 9854.
**UPPER HUTT:** *i:* 6 Main Street ☎ 527 2141. Food: All types of outlets.
Accom: Motor camp; motel 4; hotel 2. Bicycle Shop: *Cycle Centre, 15 Main St ☎ 528 0880.
Not a complete list of suburbs, ie Johnsonville, Tawa & Plimmerton.

**DIRECTIONS:** Due to the hills, heavy traffic and size of Wellington, it is recommended to take a
suburban train whenever possible. If travelling to/from Bulls, they run between Paraparaumu and
Wellington. If going to/from Napier, they go between Upper Hutt and Wellington. The fare for bikes is
up to about $4 and off-peak is the best time to travel. See www.transmetro.co.nz for details.
**NORTH** from Bulls. The terrain between Paraparaumu and Wellington is flat at each end, with the
middle bit between Pukerua Bay and SH 1/2 intersection being mostly moderate rolling. There are
occasional longer, steeper sections, like the drop through Ngauranga Gorge to Wellington Harbour.
   Those who cycle all the way can expect to encounter heavy traffic. Try to avoid using this route, some
claim it is the most dangerous stretch of highway in New Zealand. Cyclists are prohibited on the
motorway between Porirua and Johnsonville. An Alternative route goes between Brown Owl and
Waikanae over Akatarawa Saddle (see page 61).
**EAST** to Napier. This is a much kinder route than through the northern suburbs. It is probably best to
go between downtown and the Picton Ferry Terminal along Jervois and Customhouse Quays then after
Wellington Railway Station, Waterloo and Aotea Quays. After Picton Ferry Terminal it is flat along the
harbour, then SH 2 gently climbs through the Hutt Valley on Western Hutt Road. There is also a cycle
trail alongside the Hutt River, but some gates may be locked, see Attractions above.

# 15. WELLINGTON - BULLS - WANGANUI or WOODVILLE.

| **ROUTE:** | SH 1 | SH 3 |
|---|---|---|
| 15a) WELLINGTON - BULLS | 148 km | |
| 15b) WOODVILLE - BULLS - WANGANUI | | 101 km |

**LINK ROAD** 15a) i WAIKANAE (SH 1) - AKATARAWA SADDLE - UPPER HUTT (SH 2). This can be
used as an alternative to SH 1 to go to/from Wellington (Page 61).
          ii LEVIN - PALMERSTON NORTH on SH 57 and ii PALMERSTON NORTH - MANGAWEKA.
   These can be combined to provide an alternative to SH 1. (Page 61/62)
**SIDE TRIPS** 15a) To several beach resorts off SH 1 between Bulls & Wellington.

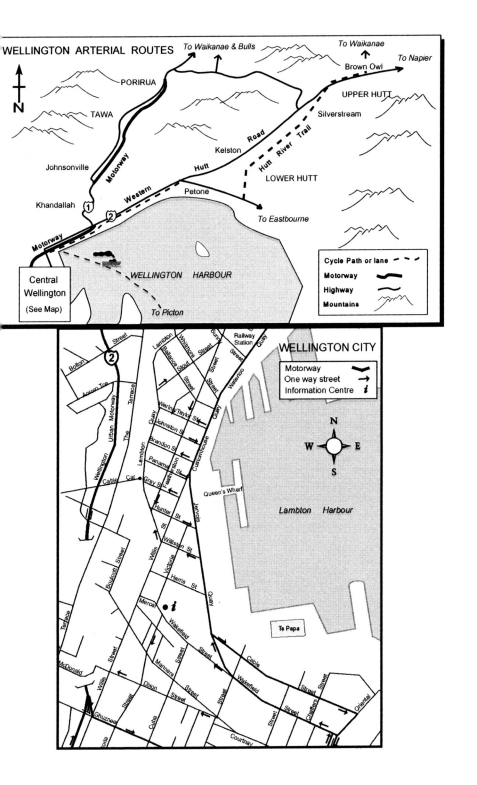

## 15a. WELLINGTON - LEVIN - BULLS.    148km

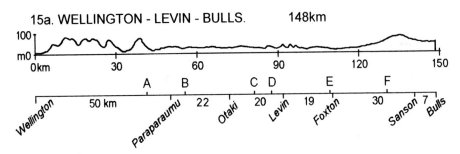

**SERVICES: WELLINGTON:** See previous section.

**A) PAEKAKARIKI:** Store, tearooms, takeaways, pub, motor camp; bkpr hostel; motel.

**PARAPARAUMU:** Alt 30m, pop 3000. Food: Store, tearooms, takeaways, pub.
Accom: Motor camp (2 km N); bkpr hostel (at the beach); motel 6 (4 at the beach).
Transport: Terminus for suburban trains to/from Wellington.
Bicycle Shop: *On yer Bike,130 Rimu Rd ☎ 04 297 2597.

**B) WAIKANAE:** Pop 5000. Food: All types of outlets. Accom: Motor camp, motel 4, hotel.

**OTAKI:** Alt 30m, pop 4500. Food: All types of outlets.
Accom: Beach motor camp; bkpr hostel; motel 2; hotel.

**C) MANAKAU:** Motor camp, hotel. **D) OHAU:** Store.

**LEVIN:** Alt 20m, pop 17,000. *i:* Regent Court, Oxford St ☎ 06 368 7148. Food: All types of outlets.
Accom: Motor camp 2 (one at Waitarere Beach); motel 8. Bicycle Shop: *Chainey's, 241 Oxford St ☎
06 368 4102. *Southend Cycles, 155 Oxford St ☎ 06 368 5459. **E) MANAWATU RIVER:** picnic area.

**FOXTON:** Alt 20m, pop 2800. *i:* Main St ☎ 363 8940. Food: All types of outlets except supermarket.
Accom: Beach motor camp; motel 2 (one at the beach); hotel 2.
Bicycle Shop: Dustins Cycles, Hall St ☎ 06 363 7401. **F) ORUA DOWNS:** picnic area.

**BULLS: & SANSON:** See next page.

**GRADIENTS:** Note: Consider taking the suburban train to Paraparaumu from Wellington or leave
the city up Hutt Valley and over the Akatarawa Saddle to Waikanae, see Options next page.
   On leaving the city there are some quite long and steep hills while passing through the suburbs,
becoming flatter after Pukerua Bay, 15km before Paraparaumu. Mostly gentle undulations all the way
from Paraparaumu to Bulls with an occasional rolling stretch but nothing too serious.

**ATTRACTIONS:** After the suburbs pass through mostly farming country on the way to Bulls. This
stretch of coastline is called Kapiti Coast, named after the Island off Paraparaumu Beach, which is a
bird and marine sanctuary, with limited access. At Otaki, the beautiful Rangiatea Church was built in
1850, incorporating huge totara pillars taken from the forest that once covered the region. It was said
to be one of the finest Maori churches in New Zealand - until an arsonist burnt it down in 1995. In 2003
a faithful replica was opened on the same site. Nearby is Otaki Gorge Scenic Reserve, is in the foothills
of the Tararua Ranges that run all the way from Palmerston North to Wellington. Several tramping
tracks are located in the forest park.
   Levin is the main centre of the Horowhenua, nearby Lake Papaitonga Scenic & Historical Reserve
was a scene of a victory by the Maori chief Te Rauparaha over a local tribe where much slaughter took
place. Foxton has Foxton Fizz, NZ's last independent soft drink factory. There are several beach resorts
each one a few km to the west along the coast. At the Waitarere Beach is the remains of the Hydrabad
ship wreck. Bulls and Sanson are at major road junctions, nearby is Ohakea Airbase with its museum.

**)PTIONS: LINK ROAD i** WAIKANAE - AKATARAWA ROAD - UPPER HUTT. Distance: 36 km.
'his route is an alternative to SH 1 if cycling all the way into/out of Wellington. Although the upper
:aches are very narrow with sharp bends in places it should be less stressful than going through the
orthern suburbs. Hopefully! The nearest motor camp to Wellington is at Lower Hutt.
Undulates and rolls predominately uphill for 6 km then climbs quite steep for 6 km to Akatarawa
;addle (440m). Then a steady gradual descent for 4½ km easing to rolling for 6 km. Two more variable
(eep hills of 2 & 1 km respectively before levelling out for the final 5 km to SH 2. Go right, passing
|pper & Lower Hutt on the way into Wellington.
VAIKANAE: See above. CLOUSTONVILLE PARK: Domain camping (toilets, water).
IRCHVILLE: picnic area (toilet, water, table). BROWN OWL: Dairy, takeaways.

**.INK ROAD ii** LEVIN - PALMERSTON NORTH on SH 57. Distance 50 km.
Gentle gradients most of the way from Palmerston North to Levin. Not much of interest, the area was
)unded on cultivating flax and forestry, now predominantly farming. Yawn!
ALMERSTON NORTH: See above. TOKOMARU: Pop 600, store, takeaways.
HANNON: Alt 20m, pop 1700. Store, tearooms, takeaways, hotel. LEVIN: See page 60.

**IDE TRIPS** To several beach resorts between Wellington & Bulls. Namely RAUMATI,
ARAPARAUMU, WAIKANAE, TE HORO, OTAKI, WAIKAWA, HOKIO, WAITARERE, FOXTON,
IMATANGI, & TANGIMOANA BEACHES. Many have food and accommodation available. Some are
illy developed, some with only basic facilities. Most are usually busy during summer school holidays.

## 15b. WOODVILLE - PALMERSTON NORTH - BULLS - WANGANUI 101km

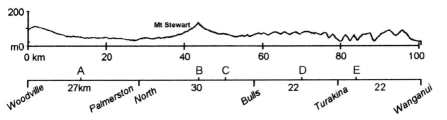

**ERVICES: WOODVILLE:** See page 55 going to/from south or 53 if going to/from north.
**ANAWATU GORGE:** Several rest areas.
**) ASHURST:** Store, takeaways, pub, Domain camping, Sept - May (toilet, water, tables).
**ALMERSTON NORTH:** Alt 30m, pop 72,000. *i:* The Square ☎ 06 358 5002.
>od: All types of outlets. Accom: Motor camp; bkpr hostel 3; motel lots; hotel 5.
·ansport: Trains stop operating at the end of September. Bus & shuttles to/from Wellington, Auckland,
ew Plymouth & Napier. Bicycle Shop: Pedal Pushers Cyclery, 303 Church St ☎ 06 356 7987.
**) MT STEWART:** Alt 135m, picnic area.
**) SANSON:** Alt 50m, pop 500. Food: All types of outlets except supermarket.
ccom: Bkpr hostel; motel 2; hotel.
**ULLS:** Alt 50m, pop 2000. *i:* 104 Bridge St ☎ 06 322 0055.
>od: All types of outlets except supermarket. Accom: Motor camp; motel; hotel.
·ansport: Bus & shuttles to/from most places south of Auckland.

**D) DUDDINGS LAKE:** motor camp (small shop, no cabins).
**TURAKINA:** Alt 35m. Dairy, takeaways, pub. Domain camping (water, coin shower, toilets) at Koitiata Beach 8½ km SW off SH 3. **E) WHANGAEHU:** picnic area.
**WANGANUI:** Alt 10m, pop 40,000. *i:* 101 Guyton St ☎ 06 349 0508.
Food: All types of outlets. Accom: Motor camp 2; hostel (bkpr 2); motel many; hotel 5.
Transport: Bus & shuttle to/from Auckland, New Plymouth, Wellington & Napier.
Bicycle Shop: *Wanganui Cycle Centre, 199 Victoria Ave ☎ 06 345 5715. *Gonville Cycles, 106 Alma Rd ☎ 06 344 4238. *Bike Shed, 70 Ridgway St, ☎ 06 345 5500. Not a complete list of cycle shops.

# GRADIENTS: If coming from Wellington go left (west) at Sanson to Wanganui, or right (East) to
go to Palmerston North and Woodville.

A gentle descent from Woodville as the road wends its way down through the narrow Manawatu Gorge to Ashurst then almost flat to Palmerston North. After Palmerston North it is mostly gentle undulations except one hill of note at Mt Stewart, all the way to Bulls. Continues similar becoming predominantly undulating with occasional longer, steeper rolls all the way through to Wanganui.

# ATTRACTIONS: The scenic gem of the district is the sperctacular Manawatu Gorge, a narrow gap
between the Tararua and Ruahine Ranges. One of NZ's first windfarms can be seen to the south. Palmerston North is Manawatu District's biggest city and sits adjacent to the Manawatu River. It is a bustling university town, claiming to be NZ's "knowledge city". To prove it they have a science centre, Massey University and lots of sheep and cows in the fields. Pass Mt Stewart on the way to Bulls, which has an interesting name and is on a major road junction.

Beyond Bulls there are a couple of small beach resorts several km off SH 3; Bulls to Tangimoana and Turakina to Koitiata. Wanganui is a city of 40,000 straddling Whanganui River and a gateway to Whanganui National Park. Durie Hill Tower has splendid views over the city and on clear days Mt Ruapehu can be seen. Putiki Church is regarded as one of the finest Maori churches. A bunch of folk held a land protest in Moutua Gardens during 1995, and somebody stole a statue!

# OPTIONS: LINK ROAD I PALMERSTON NORTH - FEILDING - MANGAWEKA.

Distances: Palmerston North - Cheltenham 27 km. Cheltenham - Mangaweka via Vinegar Hill is 52 km, via Kimbolton is 60 km. These routes avoid the traffic of SH 1. SH 54 is all sealed.

Almost flat from Palmerston North to Feilding, then gentle climb to Cheltenham. After Cheltenham are some long steep hills in places particularly when near the Rangitikei River, although they are often accompanied by stunning views. Gravel between Dress Circle & Mangaweka on the Kimbolton route. These routes can connect with Palmerston North - Levin to make an alternative to SH 1 to Wellington.
PALMERSTON NORTH: See above.
FEILDING: Alt 100m, pop 11,000. Food: All types of outlets. Accom: Motor camp; motel 3; hotel.
CHELTENHAM: Alt 190m, Store, hotel. REWA: Tearooms.
VINEGAR HILL: Domain camping (toilet, water) adjacent to Rangitikei River.
Or from Cheltenham continue north up Kiwitea Valley passing. . .
KIMBOLTON: Alt 440m, pop 200. Store, pub, Domain camping (toilet, table, water), at London Ford.
PEMBERTON: picnic area. DRESS CIRCLE: picnic area.
MANGAWEKA: See page 33.

**IGHLIGHTS** (not in any order of preference):

/hanganui National Park
lt Egmont/Taranaki National Park
aglan & Kawhia Habours
mestone region around Waitomo Caves
awhiti Museum & Turuturu Mokai at Hawea

Whangamomona & SH 43
North Taranaki seascapes
Opunake, Parehaka & SH 45
Awakino Gorge
Annual Field Days at Hamilton

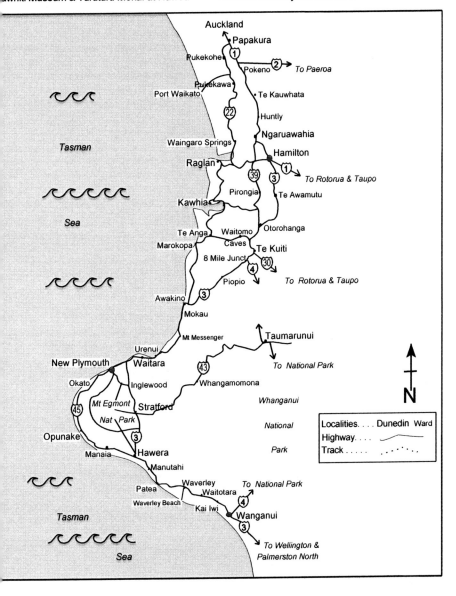

Auckland
Papakura
Pukekohe
Pokeno — To Paeroa
Pukekawa
Port Waikato
Te Kauwhata
Huntly
Waingaro Springs
Ngaruawahia
Hamilton
Raglan
To Rotorua & Taupo
Pirongia
Te Awamutu
Kawhia
Te Anga
Waitomo
Otorohanga
Marokopa
Caves
Te Kuiti
8 Mile Junct
Piopio
To Rotorua & Taupo
Awakino
Mokau
Mt Messenger
Taumarunui
Urenui
To National Park
New Plymouth
Waitara
Okato
Inglewood
Whangamomona
Mt Egmont
Stratford
Whanganui
Nat Park
National
Opunake
Park
Manaia
Hawera
Manutahi
Waverley
To National Park
Patea
Waitotara
Waverley Beach
Kai Iwi
Tasman
Wanganui
Sea
To Wellington &
Palmerston North

*Tasman*

*Sea*

*Sea*

*Tasman*

*Sea*

| Localities.... | Dunedin Ward |
| Highway.... | |
| Track..... | |

N

# 16. WANGANUI - HAWERA - NEW PLYMOUTH.

## ROUTE:

|  | SH 3 | SH 45 | SH 43 |
|---|---|---|---|
| 16) WANGANUI - NEW PLYMOUTH | 160 km | | |
| alt HAWERA - NEW PLYMOUTH | | 106 km | |
| link STRATFORD - TAUMARUNUI | | | 153 km |

**ALTERNATIVE** 16) NEW PLYMOUTH - HAWERA on the busier and shorter SH 3 via Stratford or SH 45 through Opunake (Page 66).
**LINK ROAD** STRATFORD - WHANGAMOMONA - TAUMARUNUI on partly gravel SH 43 (Page 65)
**SIDE TRIP** 16) i To MT TARANAKI/EGMONT NATIONAL PARK.
   ii Several side trips go to a number of minor attractions between Hawera and Wanganui.

### 16 WANGANUI - HAWERA - STRATFORD - NEW PLYMOUTH.  160km

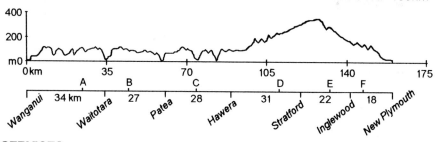

**SERVICES: WANGANUI:** See pages 61-62. **KAI-IWI:** Alt 30m, Beach motor camp (7 km off SH 2)
**OKEHU STREAM:** Alt: 60m, picnic area. **A) OTOTOKA STREAM:** W. Birch picnic area (toilet, water)
**WAITOTARA:** Alt 20m, pop 400. Dairy. Motor camp (3 km E on SH 2); Beach domain camping (toilets
water) at Waiinu (8 km off SH 2); hotel.
**B) WAVERLEY:** Alt 85m, pop 1000. Food: Store, takeaways, tearooms. Accom: Hotel 2;
Beach domain camping (no cabins, 9 km off SH 2). **WHENUAKURA:** Alt 20m,  picnic area
**PATEA:** Alt 65m, pop 1800. *i:* Library, Egmont St. Food: All types of outlets except supermarket.
Accom: Motor camp; hotel. **KAKARAMEA:** Alt 65m, hotel.
**C) MANUTAHI:** Alt 100m, hotel, takeaways. **MANAWAPOU RIVER:** picnic area.
**HAWERA:** Alt 100m, pop 8500. *i:* 55 High St ☎ 06 278 8599. Food: All types of outlets.
Accom: Motor camp; bkpr farm hostel; motel 4; hotel 3. **NORMANBY:** Alt 115m, store, hotel.
**D) ELTHAM:** Alt 210m, pop 2500. Food: All types of outlets except supermarket. Accom: Motel; hote
**NGAERE:** Alt 250m, motel.
**STRATFORD:** Alt 310m, pop 6000. *i:* Prospero Place, Miranda St, ☎ 06 765 6708.
Food: All types of outlets. Accom: Motor camp; bkpr hostel; motel 2; hotel.
**MIDHURST:** Alt 330m, dairy, pub. **E) TARIKI:** Alt 300m, pub. **NORFOLK:** Alt 250m, picnic area.
**INGLEWOOD:** Alt 200m, pop 3000. Food: All types of outlets except supermarket.
Accom: Motor camp; motel 2; hotel.
**F) EGMONT VILLAGE:** Alt 200m. Store, restaurant, motor camp; bkpr hostel; motel 2; hotel.
**NEW PLYMOUTH:** See page 68.

**GRADIENTS:** SH 3 departs Wanganui with a moderate climb and alternates between undulating and rolling country all the way to Hawera with occasional longer, steeper hills to cross deepish river channels, such as Ototoka, Waitotara, Patea, Manawapou and Tangahoe. After Hawera starts a gentle climbs for 6 km to Normanby and also for 11 km from Eltham to Stratford. between the highway roller coasters, including a lengthy quite steep ascent. Gentle up to just after Midhurst then downhill for most of 16 km to Inglewood. Mostly variable downhill from Inglewood to New Plymouth with the occasional moderate climb to cross streams.

**ATTRACTIONS:** After Wanganui SH 3 continues to travel through farming country of little interest. Access to several South Taranaki beaches is possible, each a few km off the highway, as is Bushy Park, a reserve owned by Royal Forest & Bird Society and open to the public. Patea is a pleasant little town with ruins of a freezing works down by the river. Not quite as romantic as a medieval castle but never mind. A replica of Turi and his Aotea canoe, from which the local tribe are descendants is next the library. Things must get a little cold up there in winter and a bit damp in rain!
Hawera is the principal town of South Taranaki. See the exceedingly rare Wendy Statue in King Edward Park. Surrounded by fairies, elves, little woodland creatures, gnomes and gnacyclists it is one only two in the world. Near to Hawera are the Tawhiti Museum, Turuturu-Mokai; a well preserved pa with an interesting history and scene of a gruesome encounter during the land wars.
Stratford is at one end of the SH 43 heritage trail, it is a gateway to Mt Egmont/Taranaki National Park and is also an important rural service centre. Attractions within the town include a pioneer village complex comprising of historic buildings from throughout Taranaki, and a new glockenspiel, the 1st in NZ, and very nice it is too!! Near the visitor centre is an interesting memorial of photographs of those from the district who fell during the two world wars.
Mt Egmont (or Taranaki) is the only national park to the west of the North Island. The extinct volcanic cone dominates the Taranaki Province and not surprisingly is sometimes called Mt Fuji of the southern hemisphere. There are several tramping tracks within the park, notably round the mountain and to the top, but beware of bad weather. New Plymouth is in the next section.

**OPTIONS: SIDE TRIP i** MOUNT EGMONT NATIONAL PARK:  The northern access is through Egmont Village (200m) to the Camphouse Visitor Centre (950m). Stratford (310m) is the eastern access point passing the exclusive Mountain House (860m) and going to the Lookout at 1130m.
**SIDE TRIP ii** Several side trips go a few km off SH 2 to such places as LAKE ROTORANGI, the longest man made lake in NZ and not very wide. WAVERLEY to WAVERLEY BEACH. WAITOTARA WAIINU BEACH. BUSHY PARK is a bird sanctuary. KAI IWI or WANGANUI to KAI IWI BEACH.

## 16 LINK:  STRATFORD - WHANGAMOMONA - TAUMARUNUI.   153km

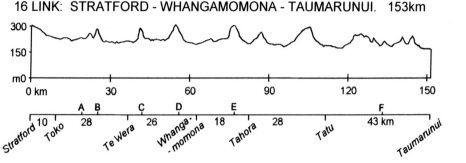

**SERVICES: STRATFORD:** See page 64. **TOKO:** Pub.
**A) DOUGLAS:** Alt 195m, Domain camping picnic area (toilet, table).
**B) STRATHMORE SADDLE:** Alt 270m, picnic area. **TE WERA:** Alt 170m, motor camp.
**C) POHOKURA SADDLE:** 280m, picnic area. **D) WHANGAMOMONA SADDLE:** 300m, picnic area
**WHANGAMOMONA:** Alt 150m, pop 200. Domain camping (cheap cabins); hotel, tearooms.
**E) TAHORA LOOKOUT:** Tearooms (also 2 cabins and limited tentsites).
**TAHORA:** farm camp (at Tangarakau, 6km off SH 43). **TANGARAKAU GORGE:** picnic area.
**F) OHINEPA:** DoC camping (toilets). **OTUNUI:** picnic area.
**TAUMARUNUI:** Alt 170m, pop 6500. *i:* Railway Station ☎ 07 895 7494. Food: All types of outlets.
Accom: Motor camp (3 km S); motel 3; hotel 3. Transport: Train stop operating at the end of Sept. Bus
& shuttle to/from Auck & Wgtn. Bicycle Shop: Paramount Cycle, Hakiaha St ☎ 07 895 8846.

**GRADIENTS:** A route for cyclists who love going up and down, no less than six major saddles
numerous hills, a couple of bluffs, a gorge and the odd tunnel or two. The elevation gain/loss over the
saddles is up to 150m, sometimes in only 1 or 2 km. Good views though and on a mostly deserted
highway, especially after it has been closed due to flooding! There is about 13 km of gravel remaining
between Tahora and Tangarakau Gorge.

**ATTRACTIONS:** SH 43 goes 153 km from Stratford to Taumarunui and is the original heritage
highway. It passes through classic kiwi back country with plenty of panoramic views from many of the
saddles, including glimpses of Mounts Egmont & Ruapehu. There is a useful pamphlet providing a route
description of the points of interest. See the huge rhododendron at Te Wera. Pass through the tiny
settlements of Toko, Douglas and Whangamomona. The latter is a republic (have your passports ready
with a small dog as the president, formerly it was a goat but it sadly died! One end of the
Matemateaonga Track starts near Strathmore. Go through several scenic reserves, including the
impressive Tangarakau Gorge and Moki Tunnel. Pass near the northern perimeter of Whanganui
National Park, see page 35. Join Whanganui River near Taumarunui.

## 16 ALTERNATIVE: HAWERA - OPUNAKE - NEW PLYMOUTH. 106km

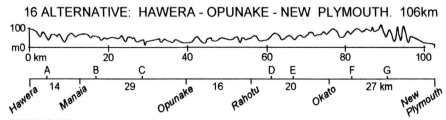

**SERVICES: HAWERA:** See page 64.
**A) TOKAORA:** Domain camping (no cabins) 3 km off SH 45 at Ohawe Beach.
**MANAIA:** Alt 70m, pop 1100. Dairy, takeaways, hotel 2.
**B) KAUPOKONUI BEACH:** Alt 60m. Domain camping (no cabins) 1 km off SH 45. **C) OEO:** hotel.
**OPUNAKE:** Alt 30m, pop 1800. *i:* Library, Tasman St. Food: All types of outlets except supermarket
Accom: Motor camp (no cabins); motel/bkpr hostel; hotel.
**Bicycle Shop: Collins Sports Centre, Tasman St, ☎ 06 761 8778.**
**RAHOTU:** Alt 50m, store, takeaways, pub. **D) PUNGAREHU:** picnic area. **E) WAREA:** Store.
**STONEY RIVER:** hotel. **OKATO:** Alt 100m, store, tearooms, takeaways.
**F) TATARAIMAKA:** 4 km off SH 45. Domain camping, (water, toilet).
**G) OAKURA:** Alt 50m, pop 500. Food: Store, takeaways, restaurant. Accom: Motor camp (no cabins)
motel; hotel. **NEW PLYMOUTH:** See page 68.

**GRADIENTS:** There are no high passes to cross but a multitude of streams drain off Mt Egmont between Hawera and New Plymouth. This requires SH 45 to frequently dip and rise, with alternating stretches of steep, moderate and gentle rolls all the way to Oakura. The last 15 km from Oakura has some particularly longish, steep, roller coaster hills.

**ATTRACTIONS:** SH45 is now known as "Surf Highway" due to the many surfing beaches nearby. Otherwise pass through mostly farming country and small communities with Mt Egmont/Taranaki ever watchful. Apart from Opunake and at Oakura SH 45 rarely touches the coast, although there are several side roads, such as to Ohawe, Kaupokonui Beach and Cape Egmont (from Pungarehu). Also near Pungarehu is Parihaka, a place where passive resistance was employed by Maori against forced land seizure by European settlers. It preceded Ghandi's similar efforts in India by several decades. At Oaonui is the Maui Gasfield production station.

**OPTIONS: ALTERNATIVE** Inner round the mountain road. Climbs from New Plymouth on the inner mountain ring road from New Plymouth to PUKEITI: Alt 380m, tearooms. This is Pukeiti Rhododendron Trust, who have a festival every November. The highway then rolls mostly between 250 - 270m before climb to Dawson Falls turn off (400m) on the south side of Mt Egmont National Park. Climbs 5 km to DAWSON FALLS VILLAGE: Alt 900m. *i:* DoC. Park huts; bkpr hostel; hotel.

**SIDE TRIP** MANAIA or HAWERA - TE NGUTU O TE MANU: domain camping (toilet, water, table). Originally a pa site that saw action during the land wars. The park-like setting has an interesting ambience due to being completely isolated from the surrounding countryside by encircling bush. It is possible to continue inland to Dawson Falls and Mt Egmont through OKAIAWA: Store, pub. KAPUNI: Dairy. & KAPONGA: Alt 270m, store, takeaways.

# 7 NEW PLYMOUTH - HAMILTON - AUCKLAND.

| **ROUTE:** | SH 3/1 |
|---|---|
| 17a) NEW PLYMOUTH - TE KUITI | 163 km |
| 17b) TE KUITI - NGARUAWAHIA | 96 km |
| 17c) NGARUAWAHIA - AUCKLAND | <u>110 km</u> |
| Total | 369 km |

**ALTERNATIVE** AWAKINO - KAWHIA - RAGLAN - AUCKLAND on various, often hilly highways, some gravel. See pages 71 - 73.
17b) WAITOMO CAVES - OTOROHANGA - PIRONGIA - NGARUAWAHIA (Page 70).
17b) HAMILTON - NGARUAWAHIA - RANGIRIRI (Page 69).
**SIDE TRIPS** 17a) Several roads go to the west coast and link with the main route north (Page 73).
**LINK ROAD** 17c) POKENO - NGATEA on SH 2 (Page 71).
17b) i HAMILTON - TE AROHA on SH 26 (Page 70).
   ii HAMILTON - TIRAU - TAUPO/ROTORUA on SH 1/5, See page 38-39.
   iii TE KUITI - WAITOMO CAVES - TE ANGA (Page 70).

## 17a. NEW PLYMOUTH - AWAKINO - TE KUITI.   163km

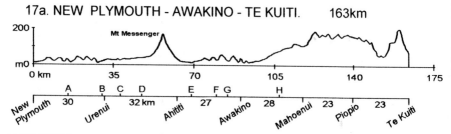

**SERVICES: NEW PLYMOUTH:** Alt 10m, pop 66,000. *I:* Puke Ariki, 1 Ariki St., ☎ 06 759 0863. Food: All types of outlets. Accom: Motor camp 3; hostel (bkpr 3, YHA 1); motel lots; hotel 10. Transport: Several bus & shuttles to/from Auckland & Wellington. Bicycle Shop: *Mitchell Cycles, 467 Devon St E, Strandon ☎ 06 758 8313. *Cycle Inn, 133 Devon S E ☎ 06 758 7418. *Raceway Cycles, 207 Coronation Ave ☎ 06 759 0391. Not a complete list.
**BELL BLOCK:** Alt 50m. Food: All types of outlets. Accom: Motel; hotel.
**A) WAITARA:** Alt 40m, pop 6500. Food: All types of outlets. Accom: Motor camp; motel; hotel.
**B) ONAERO:** Motor camp/shop/tearooms (no cabins); motel.
**URENUI:** Alt 20m. Store, takeaways, pub. Motor camp (no cabins); motel.
**C) WAIITI BEACH:** Store, motor camp (7km off SH 3). **D) URUTI:** Alt 20m, pub.
**MT MESSENGER:** Alt 190m, picnic area. **AHITITI:** Alt 35m, dairy.
**E) TONGAPORUTU:** Alt 20m, picnic area. **F) MOHAKATINO RIVER:** Alt 10m, picnic area.
**G) MOKAU:** Alt 30m, pop 200. Food: Basic store, tearooms/takeaways.
Accom: Motor camp 2 (one 3 km N adjacent beach & SH 3); bkpr hostel; motel.
**AWAKINO:** Hotel/tearooms, motel. **H) AWAKINO GORGE:** Alt 50m tunnel.
**MANGATOA & PAEMAKO** Scenic Reserves: picnic areas.
**PIOPIO:** Alt 150m, pop 600. Store, takeaways, hotel. **TE KUITI:** See next section.

**GRADIENTS:** SH 3 mostly rolls but nothing too long from New Plymouth for most of the way t Mangamaio Stream then it heads inland almost flat ascent for 15 km, climbing to 50m. Then sometimes steep climb starts with sharp, narrow bends for 3 km to Mt Messenger (190m). After passin through a tunnel near the top descend in similar fashion for 5 km to Ahititi and an almost flat downhi for 5½ km to Tongaporutu River. Rolls again from there through Mokau to Awakino.

Leave the coast at Awakino and head inland up the steep-sided mostly gentle and winding Awakin Gorge. After going through Awakino Tunnel leave the gorge. Then enter rolling country aroun Mahoenui, some being quite long and steep with a gradual 4 km descent to Piopio. After Piopio ar easy gradients all the way to Te Kuiti, apart from one 2½ km quite steep drop after the SH 3/4 junctior a climb to 200m in two steep leaps and a final 2 km steep descent into the town.

**ATTRACTIONS:** New Plymouth is the biggest city of the Taranaki Province, having a prosperou air to it, the wealth based on farming and offshore gas and oil fields. Distinctive natural features includ the Sugar Loaf Islands and Mt Egmont, the Mt Fuji of the southern hemisphere looms to the south Pukekura is considered NZ's finest and nearby is world famous Pukeiti Rhododendron park and bir sanctuary. Waitara's claim to fame is for being the start of conflict in the land wars in 1860. Thoug battles were often fierce, casualties were usually light. New Zealand's estimated total population at th time was just over 100,000.

Along the North Taranaki Bight are several beach resorts; at Waitara, Onaero, Urenui & Waiiti. otunui Methanol plant processes gas from the offshore field. Although SH 3 passes through several :enic reserves, overall the route is pleasant but not spectacular with rural country most of the way to e Kuiti. Awakino Gorge, Mt Messenger & Whitecliffs Walkway are probably the most notable. The tter is an area of spectacular sea cliffs, some km off SH 3 between Mokau & Waitara. Mt Messenger as a number of walking tracks.

## 17b. TE KUITI (Waitomo Caves) - HAMILTON - NGARUAWAHIA. 95km

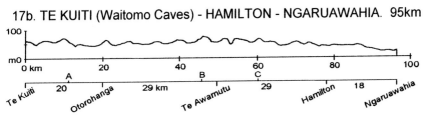

**ERVICES: TE KUITI:** Alt 60m, pop 4900. *i:* Rora St ☎ 07 878 8077. Food: All types of outlets. :com: Motor camp; domain camping 2 (toilets, water, table); bkpr hostel; motel; hotel. ansport: Train to/from Auckland & Wellington stop operating at the end of September. Bus & shuttle /from New Plymouth, Auck & Wgtn.

**HANGATIKI:** Alt 40m, motel, hotel. Turn off SH 3 here, go 8 km to . . . .

**AITOMO CAVES:** Alt 75m, pop 300. *i:* Main Rd ☎ 07 878 7640. Food: All types of outlets except ipermarket. Accom: Motor camp; hostel (bkpr 1, YHA 1); hotel.

**TOROHANGA:** Alt 40m, pop 3000. *i:* 87 Maniapoto St ☎ 07 873 8951. Food: All types of outlets. :com: Motor camp (no cabins); bkpr hostel; motel; hotel. cycle Shop: Cycle Otorohanga, Maniapoto St ☎ 07 873 8357.

**KIHIKIHI:** Alt 70m, Store, takeaways, pub, motel.

**E AWAMUTU:** Alt 60m, pop 8300. *i:* Rose Gardens, Gorst Ave ☎ 07 871 3259. Food: All types of tlets. Accom: Motor camp;; motel 3. Bicycle Shop: Davies Cycles, Sloan St ☎ 07 870 1444.

**OHAUPO:** Motel.

**AMILTON:** Alt 45m, pop 105,000. *i:* Anglesea St ☎ 07 839 3580. Food: All types of outlets. :com: Motor camp 2; hostel (bkpr 2, YHA 1); motel many; hotel 5. Transport: Train to/from Auckland d Wellington stop operating at the end of Sept. Bus & shuttles to/from most places S of Auckland. cycle Shop: *Bike Barn, cnr Ulster & Liverpool Sts ☎ 07 838 0575. *Proudlock Cycles, 135 Commerce ☎ 07 847 5744. *Cyclepro, 87B Norton Rd ☎ 07 347 5677. Not a complete list.

**3ARUAWAHIA:** Alt 25m, pop 4500. Food: All types of outlets. Accom: Motel. is & shuttles to/from New Plymouth, Auckland & Wellington.

**RADIENTS:** Rolling hills begin immediately and continue for much of the way from Te Kuiti to amilton, occasionally interspersed with undulations. At Hamilton leave SH 3 and join SH 1 going north. ie highway runs parallel to the Waikato River and flat for the rest of the way to Ngaruawahia.

**TTRACTIONS:** The world famous Waitomo Caves with their attendant glow-worms are set in nestone country, 8 km off SH 3 from Hangatiki. Ther area has various subterranean activities, :luding caving and black water rafting. Have a ride on the giant fossilised snail in the museum! Te iiti is the gateway to the King Country, another rural town that claims to be the shearing capital of the orld. The statue is of a sheep and does not resemble the ex-prime minister in any way. Heading north orohanga has a kiwi house where various native birds reside, including kiwi.

Te Awamutu claims to be "Rose Town", guess why. In the museum is Uenuku, a special carving said to have been brought from Hawaiki on the Tainui Canoe several hundred years ago, and a display of the Finn brothers of Split Endz fame. Also, it is here famous Bob Price plots the downfall of the supermarket as we know it from his Hazelmere dairy. Show him this book and get a free glass of water - if you're lucky! Hamilton is the principal city of the Waikato Province and somewhat of a cow cocky town. The climate and fertile soils help make it an important dairy farming region. National Field Days are held annually in winter at nearby Mystery Creek. This is one of the world's biggest agricultural fairs where anything remotely farming is found, including animal beauty contests. A main attraction of the 2006 event was live sex shows between bulls and a go-kart!

Turangawaewae Marae at Ngaruawahia is an important Maori cultural centre, being the HQ of the Waikato tribes and official residence of the Maori Queen. An annual regatta using traditional canoes is held here every March, the only day it is open to non-Maori.

Note: Several roads go to the west coast, see page 73.

**OPTIONS: ALTERNATIVE** WAITOMO - OTOROHANGA - PIRONGIA - NGARUAWAHIA.
Distance 87 km. Less busy than SH 1/3 but similar terrain. This route can be joined from either Ngaruwahia or Hamilton. WHATAWHATA: Pub, shop in petrol station. PIRONGIA: Store, takeaways. The nearby Alexander Redoubt is the site of the formal end of the land wars in 1881. Mt Pirongia looms nearby and the state forest has a few tramping opportunities.

**LINK ROAD i** HAMILTON - MORRINSVILLE - TE AROHA on SH 26. Distance: 54 km.
Predominately flat. Pass through pastoral country, Morrinsville claims to have lots of cows and ca yards. For Te Aroha see page 38.
MORRINSVILLE: Pop 5500. *i:* Thames St ☎ 07 889 5575. Food: All types of outlets. Accom: Domain motor camp (no cabins); motel; hotel. Bicycle Shop: Kaimai Cycles, 237 Thames St ☎ 07 889 6210.
TATUANUI: Dairy. WAITOA: store, takeaways. WAIHOU RIVER: picnic area.
TE AROHA: See page 38.

**LINK ROAD iii** WAITOMO CAVES - TE ANGA. Distance 42 km. Apart from Waitomo Caves there are other interesting karst features along this road. The scenic reserves of Tawarau, Mangapohue Natural Bridge, Piripiri Caves and Marokopa Falls all have their own special character.

Starts with a long variable steep climb from Waitomo then mostly rolls and undulates in the middle ending with a quite steep descent at Te Anga. At Te Anga go left (south) to Awakino and New Plymouth (Page 72) or right (north) to Kawhia and Auckland (Page 73).

## 17c. NGARUAWAHIA - BOMBAY HILLS - AUCKLAND.   110km

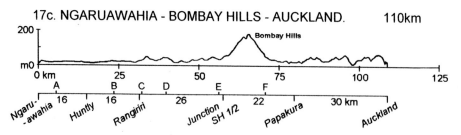

**SERVICES: NGARUAWAHIA:** See previous section. **A) TAUPIRI:** Dairy, pub.
**HUNTLY:** Alt 15m, pop 6000. Food: All types of outlets. Accom: Domain motor camp; motel; hotel.
**B) OHINEWAI:** Orchard stall.

**TE KAUWHATA:** (off SH 1) Store, pub. **MEREMERE:** (off SH 1) Store.

**MERCER:** Alt 15m, tearooms, takeaways. **E) POKENO:** Alt 60m, takeaways.

**OMBAY HILL:** Alt 180m, *i:* SH 1/Mill Road ☎ 09 236 0670, (toilets, shower), takeaways, tearooms.

**RAMARAMA:** Alt 45m, dairy, motor camp, motel. **DRURY:** Alt 20m, dairy, motel.

**APAKURA:** Alt 40m, pop 24,000. Food: All types of outlets. Accom: Motel 8.

ansport: Suburban train to/from Auckland. Bus & shuttles to/from most places S of Auckland.

cycle Shop: *Broadway Cycle & Mowers, 29 Broadway ☎ 09 298 7772. *Papakura Cycles, 273 Great

uth Road ☎ 09 298 4512. **AUCKLAND:** See pages 8 - 10.

**RADIENTS:** SH 1 continues flat and runs parallel to the broad Waikato River to Rangiriri, then adients become more rolling to the SH 2 junction just north of Pukeno. Then there is 3 km steep climb the motorway, followed by a roll to the top of Bombay Hills (185m). Leave the motorway and join reat South Road on a long gradual stepped 3½ km descent which eases to rolling country as it heads rth. Catch the suburban train (except Sundays) at Papakura.

Note: Major road works south of Mercer continue on SH 1 and will do for some time.

**TTRACTIONS:** SH 1 runs parallel to the Waikato, NZ's longest river, for much of the way between amilton and Te Kauwhata. Apart from a historic land war site at Rangiriri and orchards & vineyards ound Te Kauwhata, there is little of general interest until after Huntly, unless coal and thermal (nuclear e of course) power stations are your thing.

**PTIONS: ALTERNATIVE** HAMILTON - NGARUAWAHIA - RANGIRIRI. Distance: 51 km.

the opposite bank of the Waikato River to SH 1. Both roads swap sides at Ngaruawahia. Less busy an SH 1 but similar flat terrain and 2 km longer.

**NK ROAD** POKENO - NGATEA on SH 2. Distance 48 km. Can be busy and the traffic fast. SH2 tween the junctions of SH1 and SH27 is now considered to be the most dangerous stretch of highway NZ. Rolling to Mangatarata then flat. POKENO: See above. MANGATAWHIRI: Store, tearooms.

ARAMARUA: Store, tearooms, hotel. NGATEA: See page 73 if travelling north/south, or page 20 if velling west/east.

# 8 NEW PLYMOUTH - KAWHIA - RAGLAN - AUCKLAND.

**OUTE:** on various, sometimes gravel roads

| | |
|---|---|
| 8a) AWAKINO - RAGLAN | 181 km |
| 8b) RAGLAN - AUCKLAND | 158 km |
| tal | 339 km |

te: Includes travel in/out of Raglan, Kawhia & Marokopa but not Keritehere & Waikawau.

**NK ROAD** 18a) i RAGLAN - HAMILTON on SH 23 (Page 73).

KAWHIA - TIHIROA on SH 31. iii TE ANGA - WAITOMO CAVES (Page 73).

**DE TRIP** 18b) i To PORT WAIKATO. ii To WAIUKU. (Both on page 73).

# 18a (New Plymouth) AWAKINO - KAWHIA - RAGLAN.    181km

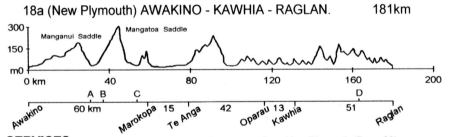

**SERVICES: AWAKINO:** See Section 17a for travel to/from New Plymouth (Page 68).

**A) WAIKAWAU:** (4½ km off highway) Alt 15m, informal camping (toilets, water) near beach tunnel.

**B) MANGATOA:** Scenic Reserve, DoC camping (toilets, water) adjacent highway.

**C) KERITEHERE:** (1½ km off highway.) Alt 15m, picnic area (toilets, water) adjacent beach.

**MAROKOPA:** Alt 5m, pop 150. Domain motor camp (no cabins) adjacent beach.

**TE ANGA:** Alt 25m, pop 100, hotel, bkpr hostel. **KINOHAKU:** Bkpr hostel. **OPARAU:** Alt 40m, store.

**KAWHIA:** Pop 400. Food: Store, take aways, tearooms, pub. Accom: Motor camp 3; motel; hotel.

**D) BRIDAL VEIL FALLS:** picnic area. **RAGLAN:** See page 73.

**GRADIENTS:** Shortly after leaving Awakino turn off SH 3 and follow the Manganui River upstream with just one river bluff to cross. Going through Whareorino State Forest the terrain rolls around the top for 3 km. Then from Manganui Saddle (200m) the road plummets for 2½ km becoming easy for 1½ km to Waikawau. After Waikawau join the Mangatoa River going upstream on a long gradual 8 km variable climb to Mangatoa Saddle (300m). A steep and tortuous descent for 3 km follows easing to gentle gradients for 12 km to Keritehere, where the gravel ends. Rolling climb to 120m then steep and winding 1½ km drop to just before Marokopa.

Almost flat as the road crosses mud flats of the lower Marokopa River to Te Anga. Rolls uphill in 10 km to 245m before descending in 6½ km to Kawhia Harbour. The first 5 km from Kinohaku are flat as the highway skirts round Kawhia Harbour rolling and undulating with some steep and occasional long climb to across low hills. Go left at Oparau on SH 31. After Kawhia village return whence you came and turn left to Raglan. Gravel starts again on leaving SH 31, going all the way to Bridal Veil Falls. The highway continues its rolling with some particularly long ups and down on this narrow winding road. Go left to Raglan on SH 23.

**ATTRACTIONS:** Going north pass through Raurimu, Mangatoa and Manganui Gorge Scenic Reserves and Whareorino State Forest, comprising of native bush and splendid views. At Waikawau a tunnel has been cut through to the beach. Prior to the road this was the only access to the outside world and was used to load wool on and supplies off waiting ships. Heading north come to Marokopa, a small holiday settlement. Near Te Anga is the Marokopa Falls and a link road to Waitomo Caves, see options below.

Next comes Kawhia, a beautiful harbour with a quaint village on the north side. Near to the settlement at Karewa Beach is reputedly the final resting place of the Tainui Canoe after the long voyage from Hawaiki. Along a 4 km gravel road is Te Puia Ocean Beach, backed by high black sand dunes so typical of the west coast beaches. At low tide are hot (or warm really) springs. On the way to Raglan pass a couple of scenic reserves and the picturesque Bridal Veil Falls. Raglan is on another pretty harbour and has become rather trendy in recent years. Nearby Manu Bay is a popular surfing spot.

**PTIONS: LINK ROAD i** TE ANGA - WAITOMO CAVES - TE KUITI. Distance: 42 km. Starts with long quite steep ascent past Marokopa Falls then rolls and undulates with a long sometimes steep escent to Waitomo Caves. Apart from Waitomo Caves there are other interesting karst features along is road. On the way pass Marokopa Falls, Piripiri Cave, Mangapohue Natural Bridge and Tawarau cenic Reserves, all have their own special characteristics. Joins SH 3 at Hangatiki.
**LINK ROAD ii** KAWHIA - TIHIROA on SH 31. One big hill to cross passing through Te Kariki & arkinson's Scenic Reserves with Mt Pirongia looming to the north. Join SH 3 at Otorohanga (going or SH 1 at Hamilton or Ngaruawahia (going N & E). See pages 69/70.
**LINK ROAD iii** RAGLAN - HAMILTON on SH 23. Distance: 48 km. Mostly rolling with a couple of ggish hills to cross such as KAREMU SADDLE: 95m, picnic area; TE UKU: Store.

## 18b RAGLAN - PUKEKOHE - AUCKLAND. 158km

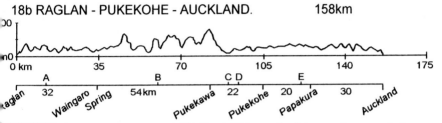

**ERVICES: RAGLAN:** Alt 10m, pop 1,500. Food: All types of outlets except supermarket. ccom: Motor camp 2 (1 at Ranui Beach); bkpr hostel; motel 2; hotel. Bus to/from Hamilton.
**TE UKU:** Store/tearooms. **WAINGARO SPRINGS:** Alt 40m. Motor camp (also shop, motel); hotel. **ANGAPIKO STREAM:** picnic area. **B) NAIKE:** The shop and petrol station has closed.
**LEN MURRAY:** Shop in petrol station (closed Sunday), bkpr hostel.
**JKEKAWA:** Alt 180m, shop in petrol station, farm bkpr hostel (3km from village).
**WAIKATO RIVER:** picnic area (toilets, water, table).
**TUAKAU:** Alt 20m, pop 500. Store, takeaways, pub.
**JKEKOHE:** Alt 50m, pop 10,000. *i:* Roulston St 09 238 4081. Food: All types of outlets. ccom: Motel 3; hotel 2. Bicycle Shop: Counties Mowers& Cycles, 135 King St ☎ 09 238 7695.
**DRURY:** Join SH 1. **AUCKLAND:** See pages 8 - 10.

**RADIENTS:** Depart Raglan and go left onto SH 22, 2 km beyond Te Uku. 5 km of gravel before aingaro Springs may soon be sealed. Basically it is rolling most of the way to Auckland with an casional, longer/steeper descent/ascent, such as at Apiatia Stream and Pukekawa. After Pukekawa ere is a long 8 km quite steep descent to Waikato River. Gentler gradients around Pukekohe, passing Bombay Hills. Join Great South Road at Drury and a return to rolling hills as Auckland nears.

**TTRACTIONS:** A quiet, scenic alternative to SH1 to/from Auckland. At Waingaro are thermal hot rings. Cross the Waikato River going through rural country on a quiet road. Pass through the small wn of Pukekohe, called the potato capital. Hmmm? When blowing westerly, winds can be a problem. ere is a regional park on Awhitu Peninsula.

**PTIONS: SIDE TRIP i** TUAKAU - PORT WAIKATO: Motor camp (no cabins). 25 km. Where the aikato River reaches the end of its long journey at the Tasman Sea.
**SIDE TRIP ii** To WAIUKU and Awhitu Peninsula. The Sunset Coast on the South Manukau Harbour. ere are plenty of black sand beaches from which to view the sunsets. These rich iron sands are ned to feed the Glenbrook Steel Mill.
**AIUKU:** Pop 4400. *i:* 2 Queen St ☎ 09 235 8924. Food: All types of outlets. Accom: Motor camp; otel 2; hotel. **AWHITU REGIONAL PARK:** camping (toilet, water). **CLARK'S BEACH:** Motor camp. RUA BAY: Motor camp. **BIG BAY:** Motor camp (also shop & tearooms).

**IMPORTANT:** NZ may be a pedallers' paradise but it isn't Utopia. So while preferring not to put off potential pedallers it is important to highlight possible hazards one could encounter.

**TRAFFIC:** Every country has its bad drivers and New Zealand is no exception. Only in the last few years have serious attempts been made to right some very bad habits, but it will probably take a long time to rectify. Drunk driving, travelling too fast and too close to the vehicle in front are the worst aspects.

If encountering dangerous drivers, try to get the vehicle's number and report it with relevant details such as time and location, at the next police station. They can trace the vehicle and speak to the owner it is better they act before someone is hurt. **A mirror is particularly useful**.

Try to be seen at all times. Cycling too close to the left may leave you too little room to manoeuvre. In cities, cycling too close to parked cars invites having a door open as you pass. Consider other road users, do not hold up traffic without good reason. Think of other cyclists who follow in your tyre tracks.

**WIND:** The wind can blow strong and hard. If it is so strong you have to pedal downhill to keep up momentum, then it is time to stop at the next location, or even turn round and go back. You're on holiday and this is supposed to be fun! Apart from the frustration of going nowhere fast it can be dangerous. There is less control of the bike and is often hard to hear traffic approaching from behind.

**SANDFLIES:** Apart from car drivers New Zealand has no dangerous animals such as bears or big pussy cats but certainly makes up for it with sandflies. Do not underestimate them!

**MAGPIES:** In spring during nesting season magpies use cyclists as target practice for dive bombing runs and have been known to draw blood! A suggestion is to draw two eyes on the back of the helmet or your head. The theory is they only attack from behind. They're so unpopular, even Royal Forest & Bird Protection Society want them declared a pest.

**KEAS:** You won't find any Norwegian Blues pining for the fiords (Monty Python types understand) but there is a mischievous native mountain parrot with a large sharp beak and curious nature. It's not into dive bombing but does steal things and has been known to rip expensive tent walls to get at tasty comestibles (food) rather than open the door. Found in all national parks with mountains and fiords!

**SUN:** Skin cancer is a problem in NZ due to the strength of the sun's ultra-violet rays penetrating the shrinking ozone layer. In summer use sun block on all exposed skin, forgetting to do so one day may cause severe sunburn, even when cloudy. Using a helmet with a peak or hat makes sense.

**WATER:** New Zealand was known as the only third world country where the water is safe to drink. While tap water is still fine, usually, care must be taken in the wilderness. It is recommended to boil drinking water because of the possible presence of the parasite giardia, a nasty bug that causes diarrhoea and stomach upsets. Even if giardia isn't present and sheep are, think twice about drinking from that cool sparkling crystal clear stream.

**BIKE STANDS:** The type found outside shops & libraries etc, where you put the front wheel. If using one with a fully laden bike then make sure the weight is balanced. Wheels have poor lateral strength and it could be banana shaped on your return!

**TELEPHONES & CARDS:** Coin phones outside cities are all but extinct. Rechargeable telephone cards offered by several companies are now available that are better value than the original rip-off Telecom throw away ones. Usually obtainable from hostels & motor camps.

**SUMMER SCHOOL HOLIDAYS:** Between 26th December and about 5th January many popular tourist locations fill up. These normally tiny communities swell to many thousands and finding even a tent space might be difficult.

**WEATHER FORECASTS:** Usually accurate regarding the type of weather but often on the wrong day.

**TOURISM AWARDS:** A company winning a toursim award may not always suggest a high level of customer satisfaction.